When Fraser Met Billy

Louise Booth

HODDER

First published in Great Britain in 2014 by Hodder & Stoughton
An Hachette UK company

First published in paperback in 2014

1

A CIP catalogue record for this title is available from the British Library

ISBN 978 1 444 76924 1

Printed and bound by CPI Group (UK) Ltd, Croydon, CR0 4YY

Hodder & Stoughton policy is to use papers that are natural,
renewable and recyclable products and made from wood grown
in sustainable forests. The logging and manufacturing processes
are expected to conform to the environmental regulations
of the country of origin.

Hodder & Stoughton Ltd
338 Euston Road
London NW1 3BH

www.hodder.co.uk

To Chris . . . My First, My Last, My Everything

For Fraser and Pippa . . . My Two Stars

I know somewhere out there, is me five years ago, someone who is facing the same enormities, despair and isolation that I faced when I gave birth to Fraser in March 2008. This book was written for that person. I want it to help them see that there is hope at the other end of what sometimes seems like a very long, dark tunnel. You can get there, I promise.

Contents

Chapter 1

Billy and Bear

It was a bright, early summer evening in 2011 and as we drove east along the banks of the River Dee the Highland landscape looked at its picture-postcard best. In the distance, the area's highest peak, Lochnagar, was bathed in a beautiful, golden glow while beneath us the setting sun was dancing off the dark waters of the river in a dazzling display of colours.

Every now and again we would pass an angler, knee-deep in the water, patiently casting their line in search of the sea trout and salmon that were now in season. It didn't occur to me at the time but looking back, I can see that, in a way, I was on a fishing expedition myself. What was that old saying? You've got to lose a fly to catch a trout.

My husband Chris was at the wheel of our car while our two children were in the back. Our daughter Pippa was just over six months old and fast asleep in her baby seat. It was our three-year-old son Fraser who was, as usual, preoccupying us. He was sitting quietly, saying very little but staring intently at the two, small photographs that he'd brought with him. We weren't quite sure what to expect from him this evening. But then, where Fraser was concerned, we never were.

He'd been diagnosed with autism just under two years earlier, in August 2009, at the very early age of 18 months. Like many boys with autism, he struggled to communicate and was prone to withdrawing into his own world. He was also capable of extreme emotional meltdowns, often over the most seemingly trivial things. In addition to this he suffered from hypotonia, a rare muscle tone condition that made his joints loose and floppy. This meant he found it very difficult to perform simple functions such as gripping things with his hands. He also found it a challenge to stand let alone walk. In fact, it had only been in the past year or so that he'd become more mobile, largely thanks to supporting splints he now wore on his lower leg and ankles.

For the past year and a half, Fraser had been receiving treatment from a small team of experts, including a speech therapist and a behavioural therapist. We'd been told in no uncertain terms that he would never attend a normal school but, despite this, we had managed to find him a small, private nursery that was prepared to take him twice a week, which had been a huge relief for me, in particular. The less good news, however, was that his moods and behaviour were still highly unpredictable and volatile. This meant that our lives were never straightforward.

Fraser is an adorable, loving little boy with a personality that seems to melt the hearts of everyone who meets him. But I'd be lying if I said that our life together had been a bed of roses, because it hadn't. We had been through some tough and extremely testing times. We never quite knew what to expect nor quite what to do, especially if we changed his routine as we'd done today. All we could do was follow our instincts. Which was why Chris and I were driving along the Dee valley, towards the small town of Aboyne, to meet the local organiser for the charity, Cats Protection.

I've been an animal lover since childhood. As a girl I'd play with rabbits, dogs, cats, horses – I didn't care. That evening I'd looked enviously into the grounds of one of the grand Royal Deeside Estates where I knew you could ride horses, something I'd adored doing when I was younger and missed terribly now that I was a full-time mother.

Our family's only pet at the moment was a cat, a rather portly and ageing grey called Toby who we'd had for more than a decade, since before Fraser and Pippa were born. It was dear old Toby who had given me the idea for this evening's journey into the unknown.

Toby was literally part of the furniture. He lay around the house, inanimate for most of the day, focused on the two main interests in his life: eating and sleeping.

For most of his young life, Fraser had taken very little interest in his surroundings or Toby. He was obsessed with anything that had wheels or spun around and could spend hours watching a spinning washing machine, playing with an old DVD player or whirling the wheels of his up-ended buggy or a toy car, but beyond that very little seemed to engage him. Recently, however, I'd noticed that he was fascinated by Toby. He would lie alongside Toby while he snoozed, placing his head on the carpet so that he could stroke and try to communicate with him.

Toby hadn't reciprocated the interest. For a while he tolerated the intrusion into his space but he'd slowly become more and more wary of Fraser, especially when he was upset. On a couple of occasions, Fraser had begun screaming over some minor change to the household routine sending Toby running upstairs for cover. Since then he'd become visibly scared of him and given him a wide berth. Sometimes now he would scamper away at the sight of Fraser approaching.

This didn't really surprise me. I knew that Toby wasn't a pet for a young child to play with, but Fraser's behaviour had set me thinking.

As the mother of an autistic child I knew I had to seize any opportunities and openings that came my way. They were few and far between, especially given where we lived, in an isolated house belonging to the Queen's Scottish home, the Balmoral Estate, where Chris worked. There were no neighbouring families and, for a long time, we hadn't been able to go to any toddler groups or anything like that because Fraser didn't cope with those kinds of environments very well. His lack of social skills always bothered me, so seeing Fraser with Toby had made me wonder whether a pet might be a positive influence on him. Interaction was interaction, even if it was with a cat rather than a human.

'I think he might like a little friend. I think it might bring him out of himself a bit more,' I said to Chris one evening over dinner. 'Why don't we try to find him a young cat that he can have a relationship with?'

We had been through so much already with Fraser that Chris, who is a very logical and grounded person, saw the flaws immediately.

'Are you sure?' he said. 'Won't a cat just get frightened by Fraser, like Toby?'

'What have we got to lose?' I replied. 'If we get it from a charity or rescue centre we can explain the situation and, if it doesn't work, they would probably take the cat back.'

'I guess so,' said Chris, although I could tell he was unconvinced.

The following day I sent an email to Cats Protection, what used to be known as the Cats Protection League, via their main website. I explained that Fraser had autism and a muscle condition that made him immobile and we were looking for a 'special' animal to be his friend. That was exactly the way I worded it, a 'special' friend. I had no great expectation of such a creature even existing.

At first we didn't get a reply. A part of me wondered whether they'd dismissed me as some kind of lunatic asking for a 'special friend' for her 'special' boy. But it turned out that the message had gone to the wrong branch. One morning I got a call suggesting that I contact the Deeside branch of Cats Protection which had, coincidentally, only been opened six months earlier.

So I sent them an email and was soon contacted by the organiser, a lady called Liz who lived twenty minutes or so away from us, near the town of Aboyne.

I could tell immediately that she understood what I was looking for.

'I've got a couple of cats that would be suitable.

But I have a feeling I know which one you will go for,' she said. 'I'll send you a photograph and some details.'

Almost immediately I'd received an email with a photo of two identical looking cats. They were both grey, slightly Oriental looking with white markings on their faces and bellies. They looked fairly young and were quite thin, almost scrawny, which made sense when I read the notes that Liz had attached.

She explained that they'd been found in a council house in a nearby village. The occupants had done a moonlight flit. The council had arrived to board the house up but one of the neighbours had told the workmen there were cats living inside. Thank goodness the neighbour spoke up because, sure enough, when the council workers had broken in, they'd found four emaciated cats, living off scraps inside the house. They would have died if the house had been boarded up.

Cats Protection was called in and they had taken all four cats. One of them, a large, black tomcat, had been rehomed pretty quickly but another cat and this pair of siblings, named Bear and Billy, were proving harder to place.

It wasn't at all obvious why Liz was so convinced one of these cats would be right for us simply from the photographs, but I was prepared to place my faith in her and take the chance. I asked her if we could set up a visit where Fraser could meet Billy and Bear and she suggested a date in a week's time when we could travel to Aboyne.

I'd learned through hard experience that Fraser didn't like sudden and unexpected changes to his daily routine so I knew I'd have to pave the way for the visit and, especially, for a new arrival in the house.

Over breakfast one morning, I got things rolling.

'Fraser, would you like to have a cat of your own that you could play with?' I said.

He looked at me studiously for a moment and then nodded.

'Yes please, Mummy,' he said.

There had been times when getting a single word from Fraser was a challenge, so three was an achievement. Encouraged by this I pressed on.

Because he didn't have the comprehension skills he needed we had got into the habit of printing a lot of pictures to help Fraser understand things. So I immediately ran off a couple of matchbox-sized prints of Bear and Billy so that he could see his potential new friends and begin to choose one of them.

Again, his reaction had been really encouraging. He had taken the pictures to bed with him each night, placing them next to his bedside cabinet. He spent hours studying them. Goodness knows what thoughts had been going through his mind as he lay there, poring over the prints of these identical cats.

Actually, I say identical, but the interesting thing was that he could immediately tell the difference between the pair. To my eyes, they were so similar that I had to write their names on the back of the pieces of paper to distinguish them. But Fraser knew which was which and repeatedly explained that 'this is Billy and this is Bear'. Autism has so many quirks and complications to it – Fraser could barely walk and couldn't communicate properly but he could tell the difference between these two doppelgänger cats.

With this first objective out of the way, I then started to prepare him for our visit to Aboyne.

This again was a big deal because we'd never really been to a stranger's house before. Fraser got so apprehensive in unfamiliar surroundings that it often triggered panics. And even if he was happy in a new environment, he would always find something to fixate on and make life difficult. So we'd basically avoided visiting strangers with him since he was a baby. The only people we felt safe going to see were his grandparents, Chris's mum and her partner, who lived on the northeast coast of Scotland, and my mum and dad, who lived in Essex.

After a week of preparation, I was fairly confident that Fraser understood what was about to happen. We were going to see these two cats and if we liked them, one of them would come to live with us. As a final precaution to head off any meltdowns we'd told him that we were going to go on a Friday after Chris had finished work, which was often early, sometime around lunchtime. We wanted him to be prepared for the change in the normal, late afternoon routine.

As it turned out, we set off a little later than planned and the sun was beginning to dip behind the mountains as we drove across the River Dee at the nearby town of Ballater and headed east towards Aboyne.

Sitting in the car, my mind was racing. There was nothing too unusual in that. There were times when I wondered whether I had turned into the world's most neurotic mother. But the truth of the matter was that as the parent of an autistic child I constantly had something to be anxious about. This evening the list of worries could have been as long as the River Dee. What if he didn't like or was frightened by Liz? What if he didn't like the look of her house? What if he was upset by a noise in the house? What if he didn't like the cats? I didn't know if the cats were inside or outside. How would he react to a cat inside a pen? In his autistic mind, cats, like Toby, were free to roam where they wanted, as and when they pleased. How would he feel about a cat being hemmed in? What if he just didn't want to know and wouldn't even get out of the car, which was entirely possible, probable in fact? On more than one occasion we had driven somewhere only for Fraser to start waving his arms, shouting 'no, no, no'. We'd been forced to simply turn around and head home. Was that going to happen again? There were so many worries fighting with each other for a space in my head. Thank goodness I'd had the glorious Highland landscape to distract me.

The dying embers of the sun had dipped behind the mountains by the time we arrived at Liz's house. As Chris pulled up Fraser was sitting forward in his seat, arching his neck to survey the scene.

'Is this where the cats live, Mummy?' he said.

I looked at Chris without having to say a word. It was one of the longest, most coherent sentences we'd ever heard Fraser speak.

'Yes, Fraser,' I reassured him.

As Chris parked up, I leaned over to check on Pippa. She was, in many ways, the polar opposite of Fraser. Travelling with her brother was always a challenge whereas with her it was a piece of cake, as she'd proven again this evening. She was still snoozing happily in her car seat so we decided to leave her there for what Chris and I assumed would be a pretty brief visit. We'd parked near the house so we weren't wandering too far from view.

No sooner had we got Fraser out of the car than

Liz appeared at the door waving. I'd had a number of email exchanges with her in the preceding week and it was clear that she was well prepared because she immediately made a bee-line for Fraser.

'Hello, you must be Fraser, would you like to come and see the cats?' she said.

I held my breath for a second. More often than not, Fraser didn't interact with people he hadn't met before. If he felt uncomfortable or at all worried, he would refuse to make eye contact and start doing something to distract himself from the unwanted intrusion into his world. But that didn't happen today.

'Yes please,' he said, looking Liz straight in the eye.

There was no question he was engaged. There was no shuffling around or looking disinterested. He still had the photo of the two cats in his hands. Chris and I looked at each other. We didn't need to exchange any words. We knew something unusual was happening.

Liz explained to us that the cats were outside in a covered cattery area, which was a mixed blessing. On the one hand, I could forget about those anxieties about Fraser spotting a washing machine or a toaster and becoming so fixated on it that he forgot all about the cats. But at the same time, I was now worried about his reaction to seeing two cats in a pen. He was used to seeing Toby having the free run of our house.

It was the sort of small detail that wouldn't bother 99.99 per cent of children. But Fraser wasn't part of the 99.99 per cent.

My anxieties proved short-lived. Liz led us towards two large pens, lined with wire mesh. One was empty but in the other were two cats that were familiar from the photographs. Bear and Billy. They looked even more alike in the flesh and I really couldn't tell them apart.

'I'm going to go inside there now, Fraser, OK?' Liz said. He nodded, transfixed by the two cats.

For a moment or two, Chris and I stood alongside Fraser, looking into the pen.

There was a raised platform where the two cats were lying down. One was half asleep and was facing in the other direction but the other one was sitting bolt upright, looking intrigued at the new arrivals.

'This is Bear,' Liz explained, pointing at the disinterested one. 'And this is Billy.'

At that precise moment, the second cat immediately sprang on to Liz's shoulder. He then jumped off and went straight to where Fraser was standing at the wire mesh. Fraser didn't flinch, quite the opposite. He stood there smiling, fascinated by what he was seeing.

'Would you like to come in and say hello to Billy, Fraser?' Liz said.

'Yes,' he said. 'Mummy will you come with me?'

Again, Chris and I exchanged a fleeting look that spoke volumes. For other parents this might have seemed like nothing but to us, the parents of a boy who had spent the previous three years being frightened of everything, it was very exciting. What happened next, however, was beyond exciting. To me, it was mind-blowing.

Inside the pen, Fraser immediately sat down on the floor. The anxious mother in me immediately thought to herself *there's cat hair everywhere, what if his asthma flares up?* But there was no time for me to over-analyse things. Before I knew it Billy had strolled straight over to Fraser and plonked himself on top of him, landing on his chest.

Liz had clearly done a good job in feeding him since he'd arrived because now Billy was quite a big cat. The move came as a bit of a shock to Fraser who was nudged backwards by the weight. For a moment he just sat there, not quite sure what to make of what had just happened to him. In normal circumstances, I would have expected a bellowing scream. But I knew already these weren't ordinary circumstances. There was no noise, no bad reaction. Nothing.

Instinctively, Billy seemed to sense that Fraser wasn't quite comfortable so he slid off his chest and adjusted his position so that his body weight wasn't pressing on him anymore, just his front paws. He then extended his neck as far it could go so that he could nuzzle his head close to Fraser's. The pair then sat there, cuddling each other quietly, as if there was no one else in the world but them.

I was stunned. In many ways, I couldn't believe what I was seeing.

'It looks like Billy has already chosen you,' Liz said, cutting through the silence.

Liz, Chris and I exchanged smiles. Again, no one needed to speak.

Fraser and Billy sat there for a couple of minutes, getting to know each other before Liz broke the ice.

'Would you like Billy to come home with you Fraser?' she said.

'Yes please,' he replied.

'All right, well I will talk to your mum and dad and we will get it sorted out,' she said.

She let them sit there for another minute or two before Chris said he needed to pop to the car to check on Pippa.

'I think we'll need to head home soon, unfortunately,' I said to Liz. 'So what happens next?'

'I will have him checked and treated at the vets,' she said. 'Then he'll be ready to move in.'

'We are moving house soon which might have a bearing on when that happens,' I said.

'Let's talk on Monday, shall we?' she said.

'Fine,' I replied, hoping everything would work out for the best.

I was worried that Fraser might be upset by the fact Billy wasn't coming with us immediately but when we explained the situation he took it in his stride, just like everything else this evening.

'Chris, you do think Liz believed us when we said Fraser was autistic?' I said as we began the return journey.

He just laughed.

'Well to look at him tonight you wouldn't have known there was a problem at all,' I said. It was true.

As usual, we had been fully prepared to turn around without even stepping out of the car. But we hadn't seen any of Fraser's more extreme behaviour. He had coped with everything, from visiting a stranger's house to having a cat plonk itself on top of him. Within the context of our life with Fraser, it felt like a minor miracle. Our hunch had paid off. Perhaps we'd landed our trout.

On the way to Liz, Fraser had sat in his chair in the back of the car, as quiet as a mouse, lost in his own thoughts. Heading home he was transformed and talked animatedly all the way.

'Billy is going to be Fraser's friend,' he said at one point, holding up the photo.

'That's right Fraser,' I replied, catching his eye in the rear view mirror.

'Billy is going to be Fraser's very best friend,' he said.

Out of the mouths of babes. None of us could have had any idea how profound those words would turn out to be.

Chapter 2

Arrivals

As it turned out, Fraser and Billy were reunited sooner than we expected.

The original plan was to wait six weeks, until early August, when Liz would bring him to us. That was when we were due to relocate from our home for the past two years to a much more suitable place in a modern house in Easter Balmoral, on the edge of the Balmoral Estate, half a dozen miles away from our current isolated position. When I'd spoken to Liz on the Monday after our trip to Aboyne she'd recommended that we wait until we were settled in the new house before introducing Billy into the family. She thought that it might be disconcerting for him to have to get used to two new homes in such a short space of time.

Surprisingly, Fraser handled this pretty well. In the days after our trip to see Billy and Bear, he had been very excited about his new pal arriving. With Fraser, excitement could easily become anxiety. But we'd learned through experience that the key to managing this was to reassure him about things at the start of each day. So each morning, before he raised the subject himself, we would remind him of what we'd said.

'Yes, Billy will come to the new house,' he would repeat, sometimes to himself.

He'd also kept his pictures of Billy and Bear by the side of his bed and regularly lay there looking at them at bedtime. That seemed to be enough for him. He was content to wait.

As it turned out, it was Liz who couldn't. About ten days after our trip to her house, she called unexpectedly. My first reaction was to panic and think there was something wrong. In fact, she was taking in a large number of cats in the next few days and was wondering whether she could bring Billy over sooner.

'Well we'd be happy to do that, as long as you are happy,' I said, mindful of what she'd said previously.

'I think he can cope with it. He's a big personality, as you saw,' she said. 'I will need you to fill out some paperwork,' she said. 'Can I bring him over in a couple of days time?'

'Of course,' I said.

And so it was that Liz and Billy arrived on the afternoon of June 27th 2011. It is a day that still lives in my memory, for all sorts of reasons.

Fraser had been at nursery that morning so Liz had agreed to come in the afternoon. When we'd told him about the change of plan he'd been really excited and hadn't stopped talking about it.

'Billy's coming, Billy's coming,' he kept saying.

Ordinarily, the sound of an unfamiliar engine in the drive outside or an unexpected knock on the front door would send Fraser into a tailspin. There had been times when he'd crouched in the kitchen with his hands over his ears waiting for the postman to deliver his letters and leave. But when he heard a car pulling up late that afternoon he headed straight for the window.

'It's Billy.'

Liz appeared at the door with a white, metal cage with fleecy bedding inside and a sliding rod that allowed the lid to flap up. It reminded me of a neighbour who had bred Siamese cats which she'd taken to cat shows around the country when I was a child. I'd spent hours in her house, playing with her litters of kittens and always saw these smart travel cages.

Fraser was fascinated and was eagerly trying to spot Billy inside the carrier.

'Billy's in the cage, Billy's in the cage,' he said excitedly as Liz brought it into the living room and began to remove the rod to lift the flap.

'Billy might want to run around and explore the house when he comes out,' I told Fraser. He was a cat, after all, and was more than likely to head off investigating his new territory.

But Fraser was too fixated on the cage from where his new friend was about to emerge to listen to me.

I can still see what happened next in my mind's eye. It was as if Billy had lived with us all his life. It was as if it was his home. As Liz opened the flap he just jumped out of the cage, took a cursory look around the living room then headed straight to Fraser.

Liz and I exchanged another meaningful look. Within moments, Fraser and Billy had started interacting together.

It was obvious they had both learned from the experience at Liz's house because this time Fraser made the first move, bending down to say 'hi'. He then leaned down so that Billy was close enough to start rubbing his face. Within moments they were lying horizontally on the carpet next to each other, stroking and caressing each other's faces just as they'd done in Aboyne.

It was a bright, very sunny afternoon and the light was pouring in through the window which gave me a chance to take a closer look at Billy. He was an unusual looking cat. His coat was a very luxurious, powdery grey colour with a v-shaped white marking in the centre of his face running from his mouth and nose between his eyes. He had white patches on his chest and on the base of his feet, like little white boots. He also had a strange, skin-coloured mark on his nose and on his paws. It was as if he'd been gouged or scratched but on closer inspection I could see that it was natural. He just didn't have any hair there. It was obvious he was still very young and boisterous from the way he rolled around with Fraser.

Liz and I just sat there, transfixed, watching the pair of them for a minute or so. We didn't say a word. Again, I think we both knew that something very special was happening.

After a while I invited her into the kitchen for a cup of tea and to finish the paperwork that she'd brought with her. We were still ploughing through all the release forms when I glimpsed Billy stalking the corridor outside the kitchen.

He had finally decided to case the joint and was sticking his head in every available doorway and cupboard. I knew that the biggest surprise waiting for him was Toby. But when the house's senior feline resident appeared on the landing there was nothing more than a bit of hissing and spitting. Within a few moments they had sussed each other out and moved on to something more interesting, in Toby's case a warm corner back in the bedroom where he could curl up and get back to some serious snoozing. Billy carried on with his exploration for a little while but was soon heading back towards Fraser.

The most memorable moment of a memorable day, to my mind at least, came when Liz left.

Fraser is not an autistic boy who is devoid of any emotion. He has got a really sweet personality and can be very warm and affectionate. It was just rare that, especially at that stage in his young life, he made eye contact and was intimate or tactile with people other than his family.

As Liz prepared to go, he just walked up to her, wrapped his arms around her and said 'thank you'. He had never touched or shown any affection or even a sign of interest in a stranger before, nor has he since. But he did that day.

I know it was a moment that touched her very profoundly. She still talks about it publicly and says that, out of all the rehomings she has done, that's the one that stands out. Needless to say, it affected me pretty deeply too.

As I watched Fraser wave her off, I could feel myself welling up. It wasn't unusual. I'd shed so many tears over Fraser. The difference was that, for the first time in a very, long time, I was crying through pure happiness.

23

From the very beginning, my life with Fraser had pushed me to the very edge emotionally. There were times when I – and everyone around me – had seriously wondered whether I'd make it.

I'd become a mother relatively later in life, in my early thirties. Chris and I had met when I was 20 and he was 25 and had been married for ten years before we decided to have children. Truth be told, we were the sort of couple who thought we'd never have kids. We had such a stress-free and easy-going life. He was an electrician and I worked as a trainer for a big firm of legal publishers, dividing my time between offices in Hampshire and in Swiss Cottage, London. We lived in a three-bedroom terraced house on an estate in Andover, not far from Southampton on the south coast of England. We'd bought it as an investment really but we had relished the challenge and, thanks to Chris's ability as an all-round handy man, we'd been able to strip it bare and make it our own. It wasn't a palace, but it was the home that we'd made. We were very happy there and had led what I suppose to many would have seemed an enviable lifestyle, taking foreign holidays and socialising with friends.

But then one day Chris had come home and said he'd been thinking about us starting a family. It was the kind of bombshell that can cause problems in a marriage, but in this case it didn't because I had quietly been thinking along similar lines. I came from a very tight-knit family background and was one of two children myself. I remained really close to my mum and dad and loved the idea of sharing grandchildren with them. When we told them and our friends about our plans they were all in shock; they all thought we had lost leave of our senses. They knew, probably much better than us, that the carefree existence that we'd been enjoying was going to come to an abrupt end. But we didn't care.

I had always been someone who planned things, so once we made the decision to have a family I had begun mapping it all out: the house we were going to buy, the bedrooms the children were going to have, the schools, the holidays, the ponies they were going to ride. What's the old saying? If you want to make God laugh, tell him your plans. If that's true then he must have had a real chuckle watching mine unravel so spectacularly.

There's no easy way of saying this – Fraser was the pregnancy from hell. In every way, shape and form. The first problem was that I put on an enormous amount of weight. And I mean enormous. I ended up being so heavy that I developed a condition that required me to walk on crutches. I am only small, five feet one to be precise, so as a result of this my pelvis softened when I was twenty weeks into the pregnancy.

This caused all sorts of problems, primarily because I often had to commute from Andover to London for work, which was a real challenge on crutches. As if that wasn't painful enough, I then developed pre-eclampsia in the run up to the birth.

At the end of February 2008 I was taken into hospital in Winchester and induced, which was when things really took a turn for the worse. Again, it was a reminder that your plans don't always work out. In my mind, I was going to have a natural birth with lovely, ethereal music playing and everybody smiling as my beautiful baby emerged grinning from ear to ear. It was all going to be fine and dandy. But, of course, the reality was totally different.

My labour lasted for three days, the longest and most traumatic three days of my life. On the second day I was given an epidural to relieve the excruciating pain that I'd been in ever since I'd arrived in hospital, but it wasn't really effective. At 6am on the morning of the third day, March 1st, they decided I needed an emergency C-section and I was rushed into an operating theatre. The surgeon reassured me that Fraser and I would be fine and my labour would soon be over. That was the last I knew about it. I was given a general anaesthetic and I spent the delivery unconscious. When I came round, I was told that I'd given birth to a baby boy, a whopper, weighing 8 pounds and 13 ounces.

Given the problems I'd had it was, I suppose, not surprising that my first few hours of motherhood were far from perfect. I spent the first day of Fraser's life pretty much out cold. It was hideous. I can remember at one point I was so delirious from the drugs and the exhaustion that when someone started talking to me about my baby, I started laughing. I told them they were bonkers. 'What on earth are you talking about? I'm not having a baby,' I apparently said.

There are photographs of me and Fraser together during his first few hours and they don't lie. I looked totally zonked out. It was far from the glowing photo of a beaming, new mum holding her baby.

Fortunately, Chris and my mum were there. Chris has always been my rock, but even he was in a state of shock most of the time because he didn't know what was going on. He didn't know if his wife and baby were alive at one point apparently, it was all so dramatic. But I don't know what I'd have done without him.

The person who really suffered during those first, traumatic hours was Fraser. Because of the nature of the delivery, both of us were a concern for the doctors. They were worried about Fraser because his head was swollen and worried about me because I was bleeding so much. As a result of this, he and I hadn't really bonded. Chris and my mum had held and cuddled him but everybody felt that I should be the first person to feed and dress him. The problem was that I was either unconscious or delirious so, in the end, a nurse had to do it. Fraser was very distressed about this apparently.

I am not so naive to think that I was the first mother to have a difficult birth, nor will I be the last. But I do hope that the experience I went through in those first days isn't one that many other new mothers go through. It was awful and haunts me to this day.

It was the second day after the labour when I was more compos mentis that I began to realise that something was wrong. It was as if Fraser was born really, really angry. During the second twenty four hours all he did was scream. No matter what I did, he just screamed and screamed.

A year and a half or so later, in November 2010 when I was planning how to approach Pippa's delivery, the doctors encouraged me to look at the medical notes that were filed during Fraser's birth. They thought it would help to avoid the same complications.

It had all been a fog at the time but when I looked back at those notes it really opened my eyes to what I'd been through with Fraser. I had known there was something wrong from the very beginning. In fact I had used those very words on a few occasions to nurses: 'There is something wrong with him,' I had said, I 'didn't like the way he looked' and I'd also commented that he appeared to be 'really, really cross about something'. I got no meaningful response at the time but it's something that has become so significant to me now. I remember one nurse telling me that maybe I needed to cuddle him a bit more! As if I hadn't spent every waking minute doing precisely that.

I was discharged after a couple of days and headed home with Fraser imagining that he might settle down there, but that didn't happen. Back at our house in Andover he picked up where he'd left off in hospital – he just screamed and screamed. Again, it seemed to me like it was frustration at something, as if he was screaming with rage. Instinctively I blamed myself. I felt like he was angry with me because I was getting everything wrong. I wasn't holding him right, I wasn't feeding him right, I wasn't dressing him right. As a new mother, I should probably have been thinking about forging that magical bond with my child. But I didn't feel that, at all. I just felt like I was constantly fire fighting.

Of course, a lot of the textbooks say that when a

baby is crying you should leave it in the cot until it stops. That may well have worked with other children but it didn't work with Fraser.

I can't really use the word crying to describe what Fraser used to do. Bellowing is probably more accurate. It was full on bellowing, screaming and shouting. It was absolutely miserable and there was nothing that I could do to stop him at times. If I didn't react to him he would step things up another gear and scream so much that his face would turn as purple as a berry and he would vomit.

The stress and anxiety this caused had a profound effect on me. I am very close to my mum and she came over to stay almost as soon as we arrived home, but the arrangement didn't last very long. After a day or so I sent her home. There wasn't anything wrong with our relationship, we get along brilliantly, but I just didn't want anyone around me. I felt a weird mixture of anxiety, tiredness, guilt and probably another hundred emotions. I didn't know it at the time but it was the beginning of a long period of semi self-imposed isolation that I would go through.

My mum was worried, of course. What mother wouldn't have been? She knew that I was going through hell so she phoned me all the time. But I probably worried her even more with the things I said.

'I don't like Fraser,' I said to her one day.

'What do you mean?' she asked.

'Well, I thought you were supposed to love your baby. I just don't like him,' I said.

It was shocking really, thinking back on it. But it was also symptomatic of the way I felt at the time and my state of mind and health. I wasn't in a good place and in the days, weeks and months that followed, it only got worse.

There were times when I thought to myself: *What have I done wrong?* There were others when I was convinced that I'd made the biggest mistake of my life.

I had been happily married for ten years with a good job that I enjoyed and a great social life. Now I was on my own with a baby that bellowed and vomited for twenty four hours a day, seven days a week. Slowly but surely, my sense of isolation began to deepen.

So many of my plans began to turn to dust. For instance, I had been looking forward to taking my new baby into my office. I had been one of three women who were pregnant. The other two had given birth before me and had both come in so that we could all coo over their babies. *That will be me soon*, I had said to myself.

But during those first few weeks with Fraser, I couldn't have even contemplated it. I couldn't let anybody else hold him because I knew that he would just let rip. It was also a busy office so I knew, from a professional point of view, I couldn't bring a baby like Fraser into that environment. It just wouldn't have been right. He would have screamed the place down.

Colleagues kept emailing me asking me when I was bringing him in, but I kept making excuses. In a way I had a secret, a child that I didn't want to display to the world. That was sad. And it was wrong, as well.

But then, just a few weeks after Fraser was born, I was presented with the perfect excuse. I was never going to make it into my old office when I lived five hundred miles away in the Highlands of Scotland.

Chapter 3

Rock Bottom

Looking back on it now, I can see that Fraser's birth and those initial days at home was the most bizarre and stressful period in my life, by a long distance. And the way in which Chris then landed a job as the Queen's electrician on the Balmoral Estate was bizarre in the extreme.

It began one day when I was looking at Highland Ponies on the internet! I know that must sound extremely odd, but I was in such a state of anxiety and exhaustion looking after Fraser that my only escape was to look at images of things that reminded me of happier times in the past – and hopefully again in the future. Since I'd been a little girl, I had been nutty about horses. I adored them and, in particular,

Highland Ponies. So one day, when Fraser was having a brief sleep, I went online and started looking at images of them. Somehow I saw that there were some really beautiful ponies on the Balmoral Estate, which led me to the Estate's official website.

Lost in my fantasy world, I happened to see a link to 'Job Vacancies'. I have no idea why I clicked on it. I didn't imagine they had an opening for a stressed-to-the-eyeballs mother to look after any Royal babies who might be there. The first thing that I noticed as the new page opened was an advert which read 'Electrician Required'.

I knew Chris wasn't happy at that point in his life. He was a pretty easy-going guy, with a dry sense of humour and an ability to get on with everyone. But he was getting fed up and disillusioned with rewiring people's houses and re-fitting kitchen electrics day-in-day-out. But when I showed him the advert and told him he should apply for the job, he just gave me a look.

'Yeah, right,' he said sarcastically. 'That's not a job that an ordinary person like me gets.'

'How do you know if you don't apply?' I said.

'OK, I'll send a CV in and see what happens,' he said. So we sent the CV off and that's when the madness started.

Shortly afterwards we got an email asking him if he would travel up to Balmoral for an interview. One of the reasons I didn't rule Scotland out completely was the fact that Chris's mum lived there, up on the north east coast. So he travelled up to Inverness and, from there, down to Balmoral for the interview, using his mum's car.

Chris said the interview went well and was told on the way out that they'd be in touch. He thought nothing more of it but then, as he drove back to the airport at Inverness, his mobile went.

'We'd like to offer you the job, can you start at the end of April?' they said.

He was gobsmacked, as I was when I heard. It was only then that the practicalities of what we'd done began to sink in. Chris was told that we would be given a home as part of the job so we didn't have that particular headache to contend with. But we were still faced with the task of putting our old home on the market, packing up all our belongings and shifting them all the way up to Balmoral, an eleven hour drive away. All this with a problematic young baby to care for. It's little surprise that my memory of that period is virtually non-existent. It was literally a blur.

The one thing that is indelibly marked in my mind is the drive up to Scotland. A lot of babies would have slept for large chunks of the journey, rocked to sleep by the soothing sound of the engine and the gentle motion of the car. Not Fraser. He screamed most of the way up there. Looking back, I can see now that the car was too stimulating for him. There were too many things for him to look at.

When we arrived at Balmoral we were greeted by the head of the Estate, known officially as the Resident Factor, but known to the staff most commonly as the Factor. He gave us a tour of the vast grounds and we drove past the huge, turreted, granite castle where the Queen regularly spends her summer holidays. The snows were still visible on the peak of Lochnagar and beyond and spring was only slowly beginning to break, but it was still breathtakingly beautiful, like something from a fairy-tale. Well it would have been if I had been in the right frame of mind.

Chris then took me to the cottage that we'd been given to stay in by the Estate. He was really excited about this part of the deal he had been offered.

'You are going to love it,' he told me, describing it as a perfect little cottage in the middle of a Highland forest. 'There's even a Loch up the road.'

But my feeling when we pulled up outside was very different. The cottage was actually a small, stone bungalow, nestled in a little glade in the midst of a large swathe of forestry on the road to a place called

Loch Muick. There was one other bungalow nearby. And that was it.

My heart sank. I just felt empty. I didn't share his excitement; I didn't share any emotion at all. So I just looked at it and said: 'I don't like it'.

'What do you mean? It's beautiful,' Chris said, shocked.

Looking back now, it must have sounded so ungrateful. But I understand entirely why I said it. I had had a baby just a few weeks earlier and it was proving hideously difficult. The fact that I was now going to live in the absolute middle of nowhere wasn't great, but it wasn't the main problem. I was deeply unhappy and, although I didn't really appreciate it yet, deeply unwell.

We moved in April 2008. It turned out that the only resident of the other bungalow was a pensioner, a former accountant to the Estate, who had retired. He was a lovely man but he wasn't exactly interested in spending time with a new mum and her bawling baby.

The house wasn't actually all that ideal for Chris from a practical point of view because he had a twenty minute drive to Balmoral. He was always on call so if a problem arose on the Estate he'd have to head in, sometimes never to be seen again for hours.

During those first weeks, I seemed to be at the cottage on my own day-in-day-out. Chris would leave at 7.45 a.m. in the morning and get home at around 5.45 p.m., if he was lucky. From the moment he went out the door, I would just sit there waiting for him to come back again. In the meantime it was just me and Fraser, who bawled and bellowed all day every day no matter what I did.

From a weather point of view, that first late spring and early summer was idyllic. You could sit there and hear the water running in the river at the bottom of the hill; you could hear the birds singing. To most people it would have felt like paradise. But to me it was hell.

Fraser had me running around trying all sorts of things to pacify him, but nothing did. By now I'd worked out that he liked to sleep in two hour bursts. So he'd sleep for two hours then be awake for two hours, sleep for two more hours and be awake for two hours. And on and on it went. He would sleep for a little longer at night, but not much. The two hours when he was awake were pretty much full on for me. He'd want a nappy change and a bottle, and by the time I'd pacified him from crying it was time to start all over again.

Every minute of every day was a challenge. Fraser

didn't communicate like most children would. If you made a noise at him, such as 'peek a boo', he wouldn't respond. Ordinarily, that magical bond between mother and child is forged in those moments. But I didn't get a smile or a gurgle or an attempt to mimic me or any of those things that you would expect. He gave nothing back at all, which for me as a mum was really upsetting.

Instead, the communication from him was all one way. He wouldn't point or make a noise to indicate what he wanted, he would just scream.

'How do you know what he wants?' my mum asked me once.

'By him screaming at me until I work out what he wants,' I said.

It was true. There were times when I wondered whether I'd landed in the middle of some warped game show where you had to guess the correct item.

'Do you want this?' I would say, holding up his cup.

'*Waaah*,' he would scream back.

'No, OK, do you want this?' I would say holding up a biscuit.

'*Waaah*.'

'No, erm, do you want this?' holding up a toy.

'*Waaah*.'

And on it would go until, by a process of trial and error, or what Chris and I rather darkly called 'trial and horror', I would get to the right answer. It was exhausting.

All this meant that I was tied to that house. I couldn't go anywhere or do anything.

My only escape came when I put Fraser in his buggy and walked down to a picturesque little spot where there was a large tree. If it was breezy he loved lying there, watching the tree swaying, fascinated by the rocking branches and the gentle whispering sound of the wind rustling the leaves. It was the best way I knew of calming him. I could even leave him there and nip indoors to make a cup of tea. I know it sounds awful but I can't describe how much of a relief those few, snatched minutes of peace and quiet were to me.

At that point, I was just living from day to day. But I knew things couldn't continue like that so almost immediately I'd asked Chris to ask them to move us somewhere a little bit less isolated. He was told that there wasn't anywhere available. So for the next seven months or so, I had to survive. I almost didn't.

Looking back on that period in our life, I can see now that I wasn't well and that I wasn't thinking straight. It still shocks me when I recall some of the thoughts that passed through my mind then. I reached what felt like my lowest ebb one evening when Chris had come home from work.

It had been another difficult day with Fraser so I

decided that I was going to go out for a walk. I headed for the road that led towards the river and walked down to a green, iron bridge that straddles the rushing waters. Again, it was an absolutely breathtaking spot, a little slice of Highland heaven. But I was in my own private hell and couldn't see it.

I'd only been standing there a few moments when the thought entered my head, *Will anybody care if I throw myself over this bridge? Will it matter?*

All I could feel was isolation and loneliness. I was desperate. For a while, I don't know how long, I stared at the river and thought about what would happen if I jumped in and let the currents carry me away. Would I have gone ahead and jumped in? How close did I come to ending it all? Again, my mind was wreathed in such a fog back then that I don't honestly know.

At one point, all I could see were images of Chris and my family – and most of all Fraser. I knew I couldn't do that to them or to him. Back at the house that evening I felt like I'd hit rock bottom, but it turned out I hadn't quite.

One of the few, positive things about moving to Scotland, as far as I was concerned, was that the health visitors were much nicer and more under-standing. I had a falling out with my health visitors in England, we really hadn't got on. They just weren't prepared to listen to my concerns and wouldn't take me seriously at all. No matter what I said it seemed to be wrong or naive. It was as if I knew nothing.

For instance, Fraser hadn't been able to keep his milk down from the very beginning. All I had to do was give him a bottle and up it would come. I told them that I was really concerned and wondered whether he was intolerant to dairy or something like that. But they told me 'don't be so silly'. They also said that they couldn't possibly recommend lactose-free baby milk. Their stock answer was simply that he was a 'colicky baby' and to prescribe me colic drops. Of course, when I put him on soya milk when he was a few months old, things improved slightly.

I felt there was a very old-fashioned, 'you've got to get on with it', kind of attitude. When I mentioned his screaming they just said it was 'the way he was and I had better get used to it'.

Things improved immediately when I got to Scotland. Fraser wasn't even registered when I arrived at Balmoral but I was soon being seen by a health visitor called Jayne. It's probably no exagger-ation to say that she saved my life.

Jayne had a lovely, easy manner about her and I found myself confiding in her. She never once treated me like a neurotic mother and she always took on board and listened to what I had to say. Of course, the reality was that I had post-natal depression. Jayne knew it. Everyone else knew it, except me. I simply would not accept it, mainly because that would have been relinquishing control of my life as far as I was concerned.

Jayne and my doctor prescribed me tablets to help me deal with the depression but I wouldn't take them. As far as I was concerned, there was nothing wrong with me.

I just wouldn't have it. I would get very defensive.

'Are you calling me a bad mother?' I'd snap.

Nobody could reach me, to be honest.

As the summer began to take hold I decided I needed to take a break and headed down to be with my family in Essex.

After a little over three months of living hell with Fraser and more than two months of isolation in the Highlands of Scotland, it was hardly surprising that my relationship with Chris had become really strained. He was going to work, had the job of his dreams and was really happy, yet on the other hand I was so unhappy I was on the verge of doing something unthinkable. Poor man. He tried to come up with ways to cheer me up and spent every hour he had at home helping out. But it didn't work. It was really difficult for him; he didn't know what to do.

My mum had been begging me to come down to see her so I finally succumbed and decided to fly down with Fraser. I'd had a huge row with Chris before I'd left. I can't even remember what it was about. What I do recall, however, is that, for some reason, I had put the tablets I'd been prescribed in my bag to take with me. We'd had lots of arguments about it; Chris thought I should take them but I was convinced they were a waste of time and I didn't need them. I'd just put them in my bag in a fit of pique, as if to say 'there, are you happy now, I have packed them?'.

That first night at my mum's I went to sleep with Fraser alongside me in his travel cot. As usual he cried and cried and cried. There was nothing unusual about that nor was there anything unusual about him vomiting, which he did. I got up, cleaned him up, changed the bed and then tried to go back to sleep. I'd barely done that when he was sick again, but this time there was something unusual. He wasn't crying. By now it was about 3.30 in the morning.

Instinctively I knew something was wrong so, after cleaning him up and changing the bed again, I got my mum up.

She took one look at him and went to find a thermometer. His temperature was absolutely raging, 42 degrees, and by now he was just vomiting constantly, so much so that he had no fluids left to bring up. He was just retching.

My mum rang NHS direct and answered a million questions, as you do. They told us to give him sips of water and wait an hour to see how he was, but we quickly realised that was no help at all so my mum rang back and just went into an absolute fury.

'You are going to have to do something, this baby is really, really sick,' she shouted down the phone.

By now it was daylight and the local surgery was open. We rang and, to their credit, a doctor came over very quickly. She took one look at Fraser and said: 'he needs to go to hospital. Now.'

Mum and Dad only lived round the corner from Southend Hospital at the time so we were there within five minutes.

I'm not exaggerating when I say that, at that point, Fraser looked as if he was dead. He wasn't white any more. His skin had gone a dull sort of grey and he was virtually lifeless, hardly breathing at all. He had stopped vomiting and hadn't cried for hours.

The doctors rushed him into an emergency room where he was soon having needles inserted and being hooked up to a load of tubes so that they could start pumping fluids and medicines into him. I was in a daze. I just sat there, unable to think.

After a couple of hours, a doctor came to see me and told me that he had severe gastroenteritis. He wasn't sure how much damage had been done but he hoped they would be able to revive him. He told me that the next twenty four hours would be crucial.

I was allowed to sit with him. The nurses had put him on a special, high-tech mat that registered his heart beat and his breathing rate. It showed that he had a heart rate, just, and that he was breathing, just. Everything was happening so quickly I'd lost all track of time. That first evening, I stayed in the hospital with him. It was then, as I sat there on my own, that everything came crashing home. Suddenly it all hit me.

I looked at Fraser, lying there, and thought: *None of this is your fault.*

Until now I'd been lost in this fog, but suddenly I could see clearly. I hadn't dealt with the situation well at all. I had all this anger inside me but I was directing it in the wrong way. I was lashing out at the people closest to me: Chris, my mum and, most of all, Fraser.

I remember vividly thinking to myself: *My baby is going to die and I've had all these feelings about him. I've blamed him for everything. But it isn't his fault, the poor little thing. What has he done wrong? Nothing.*

It was the turning point, the rock bottom that I'd needed to reach. I knew I had to get a grip, before it was too late.

It's strange how the human mind works, how a crisis can make you face up to the reality of your situation. As I sat there I realised how precious this baby was and how much I loved him. I'd somehow lost sight of that love for the past few months, probably as part of my depression. All I knew now was that I had to care for him and give him a chance in life. Suddenly, I felt the anger dropping away. Everything began dissipating away. It was incredible.

By the following morning, Fraser was transformed too. They had pumped ridiculous amounts of fluids into him and, as often happens with kids, he had apparently turned a corner quite suddenly. One minute he was at death's door and the next he was on the mend.

'Babies are amazing, they can get sick really quickly and pick up quickly too,' the doctor told me when he gave me the good news that he was rallying well.

I felt a strange mixture of relief and focus. I knew exactly what I had to do. I reached into my handbag, took out the bottle with the tablets that I'd been prescribed for my post-natal depression and swallowed a couple as per the instructions on the label. And from then on, things slowly started to get better.

My mum had obviously called Chris to let him know and he'd jumped in the car straight away, spending eleven hours in the car not knowing if his son was going to be alive, how his wife was, how his relationship with her was, whether he still had a marriage. I can't imagine what that drive must have been like. It must have been absolute hell.

So Chris was as relieved as I was when he saw Fraser, lying in a bed alert and as lively as he'd been when he had set off with me from Scotland 36 hours or so earlier.

Chris had driven down because the doctors suspected Fraser had picked up the gastroenteritis at the airport or on the plane down to Luton. So they had advised us to take him back in a clean and safe environment. He actually slept a little on the journey back north, obviously still exhausted from what he'd been through.

That car ride was a welcome relief, not least because it gave Chris and me an opportunity to talk. I apologised for the way I'd been and explained what had been going through my mind. He is an incredibly supportive man and told me that he'd been really worried about me and was relieved that I'd heeded the doctors' advice and was going to take the medication. Back at the hospital I'd worried that my marriage might go down the pan, but by the time we were back in Scotland I knew we were going to be fine.

Our problems with Fraser didn't go away, of course. Life with him became, if anything, even more challenging. In the years that followed we learned more and more about his condition. But from that day on I was able to take a step back and look at those problems more rationally. At work I had always been a logical and very organised person. So I began to tackle his problems in a logical and more organised way. My mindset ever since then has been the same. It's been about problem solving, saying 'what can I do to get him over this, how can I get around that?'. That's how I approach life with him now. I have to.

What doesn't kill you makes you stronger, the saying goes, and it really is true. It does. Those early months after Fraser was born were pretty traumatic but they were also cathartic. Since then I have lived according to the same philosophy. It isn't anyone's fault that we are in this position. Not Fraser's, not mine, not anyone's. We have been dealt the cards that we have, now it is my responsibility to play them, to put Fraser first, to do everything in my power to give him a better life. And that is what I do, every day.

Which is why, three years after reaching rock bottom, I'd ended up finding him his new pal Billy . . .

Chapter 4

Peas in a Pod

Billy's arrival really was like a breath of fresh air blowing through our lives. Almost from the moment he hopped out of his cage the atmosphere in the house changed – and for the better.

It was partly that Billy was much more of a presence than Toby; he was younger and livelier, but also a bigger personality. During his first few days he strolled around the place as if he'd lived there all his life, plonking himself wherever he felt comfortable. He was particularly fond of the little utility room or washroom I had at the back of the house and I'd found him curled up in a wicker basket filled with laundry a couple of times already.

He would also disappear into the grounds that

surrounded the house every now and again, which didn't worry us particularly. We'd wanted him to stay indoors for a little while, on the advice of Cats Protection who'd given him his jabs before handing him over to us. But we realised that Billy was too free a spirit for that. Fortunately, during those first days, he never seemed to wander very far. He was far more interested in climbing the trees that surrounded the property. Through the front porch window one day, I watched him fly up the tree nearest to the road. It was very impressive, if a little scary. He was clearly fearless and just stood there for a while, swaying gently in the breeze, scanning the landscape around him like some lookout in the crow's nest of a sailing ship.

Inside the house he continued to give Toby a wide berth and steered clear of his domain upstairs. It wasn't through fear of him, he just couldn't be bothered with a cat that lazed around all day. Billy wanted to be active, wanted to be doing things, especially if they involved Fraser.

This was the other instant effect Billy had had on our day-to-day lives. He offered Fraser the simple, uncomplicated companionship that I'd hoped for. I didn't expect him to do much. He was a cat, after all, an independent creature. I just wanted him to be a friend to Fraser and he was doing that job admirably.

The pair of them had picked up where they'd left

off during their first two meetings and got on like a house on fire. They would spend hours together each day and would be like long, lost brothers reunited when Fraser came home from nursery or the doctors.

Billy had even got into the habit of sleeping near Fraser. Because of his hypotonia, Fraser didn't have the strength to walk more than a few yards let alone climb stairs, so he slept downstairs. When Fraser was safely tucked up and the house went quiet in the evening, Billy curled up in the hallway nearby.

When Fraser got up in the morning, Billy was never far away. He'd pad into the kitchen while Fraser ate his breakfast.

'My Billy,' Fraser would say.

Given the way that Fraser had refused to interact with anyone or anything for a large part of his young life, it warmed my heart every time I witnessed it. In the great scheme of things, it was a tiny little interaction. But for me it was beautiful. It was as if Billy was gently bringing Fraser out into the world.

If I had a spare minute I couldn't help watching them together. I couldn't quite put my finger on it but I began to sense that Billy had an instinctive understanding of Fraser and his needs.

For instance, Fraser loved to lie on the living room floor to watch television. We had laminate flooring with a big, square rug in the middle, where he liked to chill out. Billy quickly cottoned on to this and would position himself within touching distance. Fraser always responded. He would place his head on Billy's belly or curl up next to him. At other times, Fraser would crouch in a ball next to Billy. On a couple of occasions I sat in the room with them, sipping a cup of tea as I watched them interacting. One of the things that struck me early on was how, while they were rolling around on the rug, Billy would lean into Fraser every now and again, pressing his forehead into his chest almost as if he was head-butting him. Often he would do this while Fraser was lying on his back, almost pushing him down into the floor. He seemed to know that Fraser liked this. How? I had no idea.

This was an aspect of Fraser's hypotonia that we'd only learned about quite recently. Because of the floppiness in his joints, Fraser was very limited in his mobility. He didn't walk at all as a baby. Not only that, he didn't crawl. If he wanted to move, he would sit up and drag himself along. So effectively, all he did for the first 18 months of his life was lie on the floor, on his back. He wouldn't even vary it and lie on his front.

During those tough early months together I'd

learned to accommodate this so, for instance, when it came to changing his nappy, I did it on the floor rather than on a normal, changing table. It was the best way to avoid Fraser having a tantrum about it.

It was only when he was properly diagnosed that it was explained to us that he lay like this because he needed support and needed to feel solidity around him. So he lay on his back in order to get a feeling of contact, of pressure on his spine and on his legs. Any other position left him feeling unsupported and, therefore, insecure. Billy had sussed out in two days what it had taken us the best part of two years to work out. He was applying pressure because, somehow, he knew Fraser needed it.

'They're like peas in a pod, those two,' I told Chris over dinner one evening. 'I think he understands him better than we do.'

'We'll see,' he said with an arch of his eyebrow. 'Let's see if he understands him when he's having a meltdown.'

It was a fair point.

As Billy settled into life in our house, we had a couple of major concerns. One was Pippa who was, of course, every bit as important as Fraser within our household. We were particularly worried about the fact that Billy might spot her Moses basket and think it was a cosy place to curl up and sleep. You read horror stories of cats suffocating little babies in this way. But it was already pretty clear we had nothing to worry about because Billy paid her virtually no attention whatsoever. He was much more interested in spending time downstairs with Fraser, so he rarely ventured upstairs.

A much bigger and worrying issue, however, was how Billy would react to Fraser when he had a meltdown. It worried me and I knew it bothered Chris too, in particular, because he'd seen already that Fraser was forming a really close bond with his new feline friend. We both knew that a major meltdown was never far away. What if Billy ran away when he witnessed Fraser having a temper tantrum? What if the dynamic of this new friendship got broken even before it had a chance to form fully? We'd stayed in contact with Liz at Cats Protection and agreed that we'd wait a few weeks before confirming that he was going to stay for good. Would we have to take Billy on the long drive back to Aboyne? Worst of all, what sort of impact would it have on Fraser if we did have to let his new pal go? We didn't have long to wait for the answers.

One evening at the beginning of July, Chris came in from work around the usual time. We'd been going through a spell of really hot weather and it had been a particularly sticky day.

'Hi. I've been stuck in a loft with no ventilation all day, I'm going to grab a quick shower straight away,' he said, sticking his head into the kitchen where I had my hands full with Pippa, who was sitting in her high chair eating her tea.

It all happened so quickly and instinctively that neither of us had time to even think about the fact that this wasn't part of the routine. When Chris came in from work he usually sat down and had a cup of tea. Of course, Fraser picked up on this immediately.

He had finished eating and gone into the living room to hang out with Billy. No sooner had the sound of the shower drifted down from upstairs than he'd appeared in the hallway, agitated.

'Daddy's done it wrong,' he said, standing, rocking back and forth on the balls of his feet and clenching and unclenching his fists.

'Daddy's done it wrong. He doesn't do that,' he repeated, this time placing his hands over his ears.

I was all too familiar with the telltale signals of an impending meltdown. I'd spent more than three years witnessing them, after all. So I knew that it wouldn't have mattered if, at this stage, Chris had reappeared and gone into the kitchen to have a cup of tea as normal. It was too late. I knew what was going to come next. A bomb was about to go off. I braced myself for the explosion.

Slowly but surely, there was a build up of colour in Fraser's face. It's not funny at all but there are times when I have compared it to watching a cartoon character as it gets really, really angry. Within a moment or two he was screaming and crying and I was trying to calm him down.

On a scale of one to ten, the meltdown probably ranked as a six or seven. A nine or a ten would have involved him putting his hands in his mouth and biting his fingers so that he'd become a complete, drooling mess. A full ten would involve him having a nosebleed as well, which was very upsetting. But it was still bad enough to have made a passer-by wonder whether there were ten children simultaneously screaming in our house!

This had been going on for about thirty seconds to a minute when Billy appeared. He'd briefly wandered off elsewhere in the house but had clearly heard Fraser shouting.

Fraser was standing in the hallway with his hands over his ears bellowing. Billy just took a position in front of him and looked at him.

There was absolute mayhem going on, but he just sat there and took it all in. At one point he even brushed against Fraser with his tail, as if trying to soothe or calm him down.

Fraser didn't notice it at first, but after a while he registered him. It didn't stop him from crying but it seemed to be a signal for Billy. He circled Fraser and me while we slowly brought things back to normal.

Chris appeared a few minutes later, drying his hair with a towel and wearing an apologetic look on his face.

'Sorry, I didn't think,' he said to me.

I'd been through enough tantrums. I'd developed a pretty thick skin.

'It's OK,' I said. 'The good news is that it didn't freak Billy out.'

'Really?' Chris said. 'I saw Toby hiding under our bed so I guessed he must have bolted as well.'

'Not at all,' I said. 'I don't know what went on at his old house, but it didn't faze him at all. Pretty amazing for a young cat to be able to deal with that isn't it?'

Chris just nodded then headed downstairs into the kitchen.

'I really hope we can keep him, but let's just give it a bit more time shall we?' Chris smiled as he finally put on the kettle to make that overdue cup of tea.

He knew me well enough to know which way my mind was going.

'I know you want him to be Fraser's best friend, but you know how unpredictable he can be. I don't

want you getting upset again. Remember what
happened with Toffee.'

How could I forget.

A little over two years earlier we'd taken in a dog, a
Saluki-whippet cross that had been rescued by the
Scottish Greyhound Sanctuary.

We'd got him for me rather than Fraser or Chris.

In the months after I'd been diagnosed with my
post-natal depression, I'd decided that I needed some
company beyond a child that screamed at me all the
time. By this point we'd managed to move from the
cottage in the woods to a gate house on the very edge
of the Balmoral Estate, near the bridge across the
River Dee where the main entrance to the castle
stands. It wasn't perfect for Fraser but it was much
less isolated which was a real consolation given that
it was November and the Scottish winter was already
drawing in.

I'd always loved dogs and fell head over heels with
this one. I christened him Toffee. I still felt lonely at
times but Toffee gave me a little more focus in my life
and I'd loved taking him out with Fraser as we went
out in the buggy each day, walking the grounds of
Balmoral.

For a few weeks, I'd dared to hope that we'd extended the family and that I had company for the long, dark days that lay ahead.

But it soon became apparent that he and Fraser weren't compatible. By this point Fraser had begun dragging himself around the floor more and more. This was a problem because Toffee was moulting a lot and had left a lot of hair on the carpets. Fraser had been fine with our cat Toby but it turned out that he was really sensitive to dog hair and dander and Toffee's shedding had triggered nosebleeds and asthma attacks. They had been so severe that we'd had to take him to the doctor a couple of times.

It hadn't taken Chris and me long to reach the inevitable conclusion. Toffee would have to go back to the Sanctuary. They were amazingly understanding and found another home almost immediately. We agreed to travel down to Dundee to hand Toffee over to a volunteer who was going to take him on to Berwick-upon-Tweed, on the England–Scotland border.

The drive down there was horrible. Fraser was in his car seat, Toffee was in his bed at the back and I was in the front with Chris, feeling like my heart was being torn into a thousand tiny pieces again.

We had arranged to meet the volunteer in the car park of a big pet superstore where we would hand Toffee over. But when we pulled up I realised I couldn't face it. I was too upset. So I took Toffee for a quick walk, said my goodbyes then gave him to Chris for the handover. Back in the car I tried not to cry too much in case I set Fraser off, but it was a losing battle.

It was a grim time and this was yet another grim thing that had happened. But I reminded myself of the promise I'd made to myself and Fraser and soon picked myself up. I didn't have a choice in the matter.

By that point in his development it was becoming more and more apparent that Fraser had severe problems.

I'm sure every parent has one of those books which contain all the milestones their child is meant to reach by a certain age. There are points in their development at which they should be walking, talking, going to the toilet on their own, and feeding themselves. With Fraser, I pretty quickly realised that I could forget about all those landmarks. He wasn't going to meet them. Any of them.

As his mother, I understood that each of these missed milestones was only confirming what I already knew: that there was something wrong. But the medical profession only began to look into his condition when he'd missed so many that it began to show up on their radar as well. In January 2009, when he was 10 months old, he'd been referred to an orthopaedic specialist because they thought there might be something physically wrong with him as he wasn't making any progress walking. All he did was lie on his back.

They took a look at him but couldn't find anything specific, so they referred him to a paediatric consultant in Aberdeen, Dr Stephen.

Autism was the obvious explanation for a lot of his behaviour but we were told he was too young to be assessed for it. Children weren't generally diagnosed until they were four. As was so often the case back then, it took something dramatic to get things moving.

One Monday evening, when he was around 14 months old, Fraser was lying on the floor drumming his legs like he often used to do. But he was also going really rigid every now and again. He was then shaking and trembling. He was doing this repeatedly, going stiff and trembling, going stiff and trembling. He would be OK for a while but then it would start again. It was something we'd seen a couple of times before, but never this bad. It was quite distressing to see and obviously we were worried. We thought he might be having a seizure.

I phoned Chris's mum because at the time her job was working with special needs adults. I knew that she'd had some experience with seizures. As soon as I described what he was doing she told me to phone for an ambulance.

Of course, it wasn't that easy. Chris phoned NHS direct and was asked a load of questions. He told them about the trembling and the stiffening up. He also mentioned that Fraser wasn't coherent and we were really worried about his colour. In fact, he was really ashen by this point. Eventually they decided to send an ambulance.

The paramedic shared our concern. During the last ten minutes of the drive to the hospital we were blue lighted because Fraser's colour had changed for the worse. But he was soon in safe hands.

After a while we were seen by a specialist who said he was pretty sure it wasn't a seizure, although he didn't have an alternative explanation at that point. He suggested that they keep him in for observation, which was frustrating in the extreme. We were really worried.

By coincidence we already had an appointment with Dr Stephen, two days later. We had already had one appointment with her a month or so earlier during which she had asked us to observe Fraser and, if possible, film him. Chris had captured some footage of a couple of meltdowns and also these strange fit-like moments which we planned to show her at that next meeting.

I stayed with Fraser on the Monday night while Chris went home then returned the next day with his mother and the video camcorder.

By coincidence, Dr Stephen had arrived early on the Tuesday morning with a team of colleagues when I'd gone down to get some breakfast. Strictly speaking we were due to see her the next day, but she decided to examine Fraser there and then. Chris had been there but had gone to fetch me, leaving his mother with the doctor who began looking at the footage on the camcorder.

The doctors had watched the film three or four times, looking very concerned as they did so. By the time we got back Dr Stephen had decided that it was not a medical seizure.

'It's a self-gratification behaviour of some kind,' she said. 'I think we need to get Fraser in to do more detailed tests.'

It was a very significant moment for us. That was the trigger for the medical powers-that-be to pay attention. After that, Fraser had to have an MRI scan and an EEG recording during which they placed monitors all over his head so that they could measure his brain waves for signs of epilepsy. There were none, fortunately.

And so it was that, a few months after the 'seizure', in August 2009, Fraser was invited to spend a week being tested and observed at a specialist children's

centre in Aberdeen. It was probably the most important week of Fraser's life, certainly up to that point.

Chris had to take a week off work, which wasn't
easy because the Queen was in residence. Each day
we'd make the hour and a half drive to the centre, a
developmental nursery school for children with
special needs. The building was also a centre for
therapy and children with physical disabilities, so
when you walked in there was a very positive feel.
There were all sorts of sensory things on the walls,
wooden wheels that you could spin or bumps that
you could feel as you walk, and all at child's level
which worked really well.

For Fraser, the idea of walking into a new building
with lots of long corridors was quite daunting but
because there was all this stuff at his level it took
away the fear, which I thought was quite clever.
There was a big playroom that had a one way mirror
all the way along one wall. Chris and I were able to
sit behind the glass to watch him for a while.

Fraser wasn't the only child being assessed; there
were six in all including him. They were all under
five but Fraser was the youngest. Each child had a
nursery assistant to work with them. They were then
visited by a speech therapist, a psychologist and an
occupational therapist. They spent a week looking at
all aspects of his behaviour. For instance, they wanted
to see his reaction to different textures so they let him

play with shaving foam, jelly, sand, water and paint, lots of messy things to see what he would engage with and what he didn't engage with. They also observed us interacting and talking to Fraser, then spent time individually with him and talking to us.

There were moments when I had to laugh, really.

'You seem to instinctively know what Fraser wants,' someone said to me at one point.

I just smiled.

'No, I have just been bellowed at for 18 months,' I said. 'He never asks for anything directly. I have only learned to recognise what he wants because he's a child of extreme routine and I've learned his routine,' I explained.

To be fair, they spotted a lot of things that we'd never realised. For instance, we knew that Fraser had really good eyesight and could spot things from a long distance, but we hadn't realised that if you pointed at something he would refuse to follow the line of sight. Working with the nurses, he would not engage in that way. And there were other insights that really rang true.

Someone, for instance, commented that Fraser was more determined not to do things than he was to do things. I couldn't help nodding at that. When we drove in the car, for instance, he was absolutely determined that he wouldn't fall asleep. It was the same when he was in a buggy or a cot that wasn't

his own. It was as if he had made a conscious decision: *I know what you want me to do but I am not going to
do it, and I am going to put every ounce of my energy into
not doing it.*

It was a very odd week. It was strange watching
people talking to Fraser or interacting with him
and then scribbling notes on to a clipboard or into
a notebook. In a way, I felt guilty that I was allowing strangers to treat him almost like a guinea pig.
But we needed answers and this was the only way
to get them.

At the end of the week, Chris and I were invited to
Aberdeen to sit down with all the experts to discuss
Fraser's future. It's a day that will always live in both
our memories.

We left Fraser at home with Chris's mum and drove
to Aberdeen for the final time that week. We went
into this room with this great big mahogany, oval
table with twelve or thirteen people sat around it.
There were all sorts of therapists and experts who
had been working with Fraser and each one of them
had something to say about him. It was all summa-
rised in the bulky report that we were all handed at
the start of the meeting.

It made for pretty devastating reading.

Again, a lot of what was written confirmed things
we knew. The clinical psychologist noted that he
had trouble interacting with strangers and had a

fear of them arriving at the door at home. We nodded at that. We'd spent long hours pacifying Fraser when a man had unexpectedly come to read the electric meter.

It was also noted that Fraser's social communication was severely limited and was confined to just 25 words. Again, we knew that. But of course, I also knew that he had another 25 forms of screaming and bellowing. That was his own unique form of communication.

The doctors also noted that Fraser had issues with many of the items he encountered in his day-to-day life, his cups in particular. He had to drink out of a particular cup and would become extremely volatile if he didn't get it, they said. Again, they were confirming realities with which we were all too familiar. I'd had to buy dozens and dozens of cups before finding one that Fraser was happy with. I still had shelves full of the rejected ones at home.

One thing that we didn't know, however, related to a period when he was 8 or 9 months old and had been doing something very strange. Every now and again he would bring his knees up to his body and then slam his legs down on the floor really heavily. This had been recorded by our doctor at the time and had come up in conversations with us during the week. At the time the doctors thought it was a display of something they called a 'tonic rigidity of the limbs'. Alarmingly, these doctors now disagreed with the hospital's verdict a few months earlier and felt that it might well have been caused by 'seizures'.

We knew that the conclusions were the key thing because they would have a huge impact on Fraser's future. They confirmed our fears.

The report concluded that Fraser was, in their phrase, 'on the autistic spectrum'. It also said he had behavioural problems and put a name to the floppiness in his limbs that we'd recognised for months now: hypotonia.

As we digested and spoke about all the findings with the experts around the table, the verdict was pretty damning. It wasn't clear whether Fraser would ever be able to walk or move around properly. Therapy might help, they said, but, as with his speech, there was no guarantee. One of the consultants was adamant that it was up to Fraser. He said he was very strong-willed and would 'do it when he was ready to do it'.

The conclusion on his educational future was much more definitive. 'Fraser will never attend a mainstream school,' one of the consultants said at one point. I remember that phrase as if it had been spoken five minutes ago. It was like a stab to the heart for both Chris and I. The lady wasn't being malicious, she was just doing her job and telling us straight. We may not have liked it but it was what we needed to hear.

It was a paradoxical moment in many ways. On the one hand, Chris and I were devastated. As a parent, you have so many hopes and dreams for your child. The half an hour or so that we spent in that room in Aberdeen blew many of them away.

But I also felt a really strong sense of vindication. For so long no one would listen to me. Now the most respected people in their fields in Scotland had confirmed what I'd suspected for 18 months. All those people who had told me I was neurotic and over-reacting were wrong.

There was another positive too. Fraser's diagnosis meant that we got a lot more help to look after him. After a year and a half dealing with Fraser effectively on my own, I was given professional help in the form of physiotherapy, occupational therapy and speech therapy.

The Factor at Balmoral was also wonderfully helpful. He was always asking after Fraser and when we explained about the diagnosis he was keen to do whatever he could to help.

The gate house wasn't ideal. To begin with Fraser couldn't do stairs so, if Chris wasn't around to help, I had to carry him up and down a long, awkward flight of old stone steps to get to and from his bedroom. The stairs twisted round on themselves a couple of times as you climbed up. Carrying a child that always lay limp in my arms was a real challenge and there were times when it felt like I was hauling a ten tonne weight up a mountain.

Aside from that, it was a very old, cold, stone building which meant that Fraser got really chilly on the floor. There were carpets but there was a void beneath the flagstones which made it ice cold in the mornings and at night.

Last, but not least, there was a problem with the light. One of the immediate steps the doctors had taken, even before we were seen at Aberdeen, was to give him a special, orthopaedic chair that gave him extra support to stand. The problem was the windows were really high at home and he couldn't see out. His new therapists had agreed with Chris and me that it wasn't good for a child that needed stimulation to be in a house where he was effectively in the dark. For him it was a little prison because he couldn't see out.

The Factor was really understanding when we explained all this. He told us that he would look into another move and mentioned a place that he thought might be suitable, another of the Estate's many houses, a few miles away from Balmoral, on open land near Ballater. An elderly lady who used to work on the Estate had been living there but she had become frail and been admitted to a home.

The Factor checked it out and decided it was a no-brainer; everything was on one level, the windows were very low and it was very light and bright. It had been a huge improvement for us all. The house gave us a real boost, especially as Fraser started having a lot of therapy.

Looking back on it now, I can see that that time was a real breakthrough period for us. For a year and a half we had largely been left to our own devices. We knew there was something wrong but had no real, specialist, professional help to understand let alone try to solve Fraser's problems. The official diagnosis had changed that. We no longer felt like we were on our own and began to encounter a lot of talented people. One of them stood out, a physiotherapist named Helen.

A consultant in Aberdeen was adamant that the problems Fraser had standing up and walking were linked to his development. His advice to us was to be patient and wait. 'He will walk when he is ready to walk, he is just being stubborn,' he said. But as soon as Helen began working with Fraser, she told us that she disagreed. 'There's more to it than that,' she said.

Helen very quickly saw that there was a problem with Fraser's ankles, which meant that they could rotate virtually through 360 degrees. Because of his hypotonia and the lack of tone in his muscles, there was so much looseness in them that when he tried to put weight on his ankles they literally collapsed. It was the same when he tried to pick things up. The analogy we came up with at that time was with one of those 'win a toy' games you see in fairgrounds and amusement arcades, where you lower a metallic crane-like contraption in an attempt to grab a cuddly bear or a toy car. They are almost always impossible. The moment the contraption makes contact with the toy it just collapses and goes limp. It has absolutely no grip whatsoever. That was how it was with Fraser. So he had absolutely no chance of supporting his weight – and even less chance of walking.

'That's why he can't stand. It's nothing to do with his development, he can't do it physically,' Helen told us.

So she recommended that he be given a pair of specially moulded leg splints to support his weight around the ankles.

The consultant disagreed, unsurprisingly, but Helen went over his head. She fought tooth and nail for us and won in the end. Fraser got his splints and, very quickly, was able to stand up and take the first steps towards walking. If it hadn't been for Helen we might have been waiting for months, even years, to make that breakthrough.

What was remarkable about Helen was her aura.

She was quite New Age, had long hair and wore long, dangly earrings. She was the calmest and most positive influence we had in our lives at that point and she had a really profound impact on Fraser. She calmed him down.

All the other workers had to put a lot of effort in to get Fraser to trust them and sometimes he would take against them. There was one physiotherapist who he wouldn't even let touch him, which was a problem, naturally.

But with Helen it came instantly. She had his trust from day one.

It was now almost two years later and Helen had moved on. But I couldn't help thinking of her as I watched Fraser and Billy together. They seemed to have that same instant bond, that same level of trust. And as Billy settled into life with us, that trust was blossoming.

Having survived the first week or so in the house, Billy really began to enjoy himself and relax. With the summer in full bloom it meant that he spent a lot of time exploring our gardens, its trees and the shrubbery surrounding us. To our surprise, this had an almost immediate impact on Fraser.

Unfortunately, Fraser had never really liked going

out in the garden very much. It was probably because he found it daunting, he preferred to feel enclosed. But it was annoying for Chris and me, especially when we had good weather. One of the reasons we'd liked the house was that it was set off the road and had around half an acre of grounds, including a really nice lawn. We had this big quilted blanket and Chris would carry Fraser out into the garden, placing him on the blanket so that we could all enjoy the weather. But he wouldn't stay there; he would either scream and shout until we took him back indoors or, failing that, he would crawl his way back into the house where he'd usually plonk himself back inside the porch so that he could sit spinning the wheel of his buggy. Again, he was determined that he was not going to do what we wanted and was prepared to push himself to achieve this.

But then one sunny evening, about three weeks after Billy arrived, Chris and I decided to sit in the garden for an hour or so. The weather really was glorious and the sun was still just visible through the vast pine forest that stretched to the east. For a few precious minutes we sat there, knowing that all was well within the family. Fraser was watching television inside. Pippa, who was now eight months old, had just eaten her tea and was already snoozing upstairs. Billy was roaming the grounds somewhere. All was calm, well, as calm as it ever got in our household.

We'd only been sitting there for a short while when I saw a figure in the porch.

'Chris, look,' I said, nudging him gently.

Fraser had obviously dragged himself along from the living room, but he wasn't agitated at all. In fact he was quiet and seemingly content. For a moment he sat there, spinning the wheels of the upturned buggy in the porch but at the same time arching his neck so as to look outside into the garden.

After a few minutes he edged himself out on to the doorway and began scanning the grounds. He then began shouting.

'Billy, Billy.'

Chris and I just smiled at each other and watched.

Fraser couldn't see all of the garden from his viewpoint in the porch, so he picked himself up and took a couple of unsteady steps out into the grounds. He then began scanning the lawn and the bushes for his mate.

'Billy, Billy where are you?' he said every now and again.

Chris was about to get up to fetch Fraser's quilted blanket but I put my hand on his and told him to sit down.

'Give it a minute, let's see what happens', I said.

All of a sudden, there was a bit of a commotion in a bush to the side of the house. Billy appeared, looking a little bedraggled. There were bits of overgrowth stuck to his coat and he looked slightly out of breath, as if he'd been running. He spotted Fraser and immediately trotted over to him.

By now Fraser had engineered his way down the single, shallow step that led on to the lawn and walked a couple of yards on to the grass. That was close to his limit, so he had knelt down and waited for his pal to arrive.

'Hello Billy,' he said. He then began whispering and talking to him quietly, reverting to the secret language that they seemed to have developed.

At that point, Chris went over to Fraser and helped him over to the lawn where he placed the rug out for him. Billy, naturally, followed.

For the next twenty minutes or so the pair of them lay next to each other, cuddling and wrestling each other in the evening light.

It was bliss for us, not just because it gave us a much-needed break, but because it confirmed what we'd both noticed in the past few days.

Fraser was a typical child in some ways, in particular, he responded well to incentives. If you gave him a reason to do something, the chances were he would do it. Billy had given him the incentive to get up and move around. On a couple of occasions, he had wandered off into the washroom or the kitchen while Fraser was watching television. Without any fuss or protest, Fraser had picked himself up and followed his pal. If we'd asked Fraser to come to the kitchen or into the washroom, the likelihood was that he wouldn't have come. But the fact that Billy was there meant there must be something interesting going on that he also needed to check out.

It had now progressed to the point where Fraser was following Billy into the garden.

Again it would have seemed like a tiny thing to most parents but to us it was really significant. We were delighted.

That evening we sat out in the garden until dusk.

'Did you send Liz that email confirming that Billy's staying?' Chris said, as we watched the blood red sky to the west.

'Not yet, no,' I said.

'Think you better had, don't you?' he said, squeezing my hand.

Chapter 5

The Lost Cord

One August morning, around 10 o'clock, I grabbed the hoover and headed into Fraser's room. I'd dropped him off at nursery half an hour earlier and, with Pippa happily playing with her favourite stacking cups next door on the living room rug, I wanted to seize the moment to change his bed linen and give his room a general tidy up before rewarding myself with a nice cup of tea.

All thoughts of a relaxing mid-morning break disappeared the instant I walked into his room and looked at his bedside cabinet.

My heart sank.

'Oh no,' I heard myself saying out loud. 'He's left his cord behind.'

Fraser's red cord had been a central part of his life for more than a year and a half now.

Of course lots of children have items they are attached to, whether it's a blanket or a teddy bear. Goodness knows I'd tried to interest Fraser in something more normal like that, but none of the toys I'd bought him had fascinated him like this frazzled, eighteen inch piece of knotted shoelace. It went with him absolutely everywhere.

It was, in some ways, his escape mechanism. If he was anxious or agitated, Fraser would wave the cord like a lasso so that he could 'zone out' of whatever was happening around him. The action was, apparently, something common in autistic children – some called it 'stimming', short for stimulating. He would stand with his hand outstretched behind him and start whirling the cord around at quite a speed. It was mesmerising, even for me watching. I'm sure it had an even more hypnotic effect on him. When he was standing there whirling his cord around he really was lost to the rest of the world.

It was actually the second lasso-like length of material he'd had. The cord's forerunner was a strap of plastic from one of his buggies that he'd somehow broken off and carried everywhere with him when he was just a year old. He'd still had this when he was assessed in Aberdeen, which had fascinated the medical experts there. But since then it had been replaced in his affections by this length of cord.

I had no idea where it had come from. All I knew was that it was as closely connected to him as the umbilical cord he'd been born with.

The cord was a couple of feet long so, when Fraser had started playing with it, Chris and I had tied a series of knots in it to shorten it. Fraser often had the cord in bed with him and we didn't want him accidentally wrapping it around his neck. If that was scary, the prospect of him losing the cord was possibly even scarier. Chris and I were ridiculously nervous about it, with good cause. Tiny things could propel Fraser into a rage. I couldn't imagine what kind of meltdown he'd have had if he hadn't been able to find it.

So as I looked at the cord sitting at his bedside, I felt the panic building inside me. *He is going to go absolutely ballistic*, I thought.

After a few moments, however, the panic gave way to puzzlement. Why hadn't he mentioned it in the car earlier, I wondered? For some reason, Fraser didn't like taking the cord into his nursery so he always insisted on leaving it in the same spot on the back seat of the car when he travelled there in the morning. It had to be there, in the exact same position, when he came out again a few hours later. It was really odd that he hadn't mentioned its absence this morning.

I headed into the kitchen and flicked the kettle on. As I made myself a cup of tea and thought about it, I felt the anxiety waning slightly.

Think about it Louise, I told myself. *If he had wanted to take it with him but had somehow forgotten, I would have known about it pretty darned quickly. We'd have had a tantrum in the car and, in all probability, I'd have had to turn around to fetch it. But there had been nothing. Not a peep.*

So I decided to leave it there and wait to see if the cord had been replaced by something else. Fraser was endlessly unpredictable. Maybe he had a new escape mechanism. Maybe he'd found a new length of cord to whirl around. There was no way I'd be able to guess. I put it to the back of my mind and got on with the cleaning and the rest of my morning routine.

I had more than enough to be worrying about. We had finally been offered a home on the actual Balmoral Estate and were now only a few weeks away from moving again so shelves had begun to be cleared and packing cases and cardboard boxes had begun appearing in different rooms around the house. My mum was coming up to help, which was a godsend, but for now I had two years' worth of accumulated rubbish to sort through, especially in Fraser's room.

Sitting there, going through the boxes of toys, I couldn't help shaking my head in wonder at the lengths Chris and I had gone to in a vain attempt to engage Fraser.

Even before he'd been officially diagnosed, I had researched every website there was looking for sensory toys or other toys suitable for autistic children. None of them had captured his attention. At one point, Chris and I had covered his bedroom floor with a lino that depicted a road, with a hospital and a fire station and all sorts of other buildings. Our thinking was that he was spending a lot of time on the floor and he also had a lot of cars. We imagined him sitting there, like an ordinary boy, driving his trucks and fire engines and cars up and down the road. But that didn't happen. Whenever Chris or I walked into his room, we'd find him sitting there with the cars turned upside down, spinning the wheels. Either that or he'd be ignoring the toys completely and waving that damned cord around. It was very dispiriting.

So after a while I learned not to bother buying new toys. It wasn't because I begrudged buying them, it was simply that I didn't know what was going to float his boat. If we were out and about and I saw something in a charity shop I'd say 'I'll try that'. I never knew.

There were odd successes. One of the best things I ever bought him was a Bob the Builder tape measure which cost me 25p. Fraser had found it himself, rummaging around in a bargain bin in a charity shop in Ballater. He spent hours playing with it. He would just sit there pulling it out and then rolling it back in. That sort of thing appealed to Fraser, something with a mechanism that could be repeated, again and again and again.

But most of his toys had been a failure. As I cleared the room this morning, I looked at the bubble lamp with plastic fish inside it which I'd bought to give Fraser some sensory stimulation. I'd placed it in a corner of his room along with some really nice interactive toys that one of his therapists had recommended to help his co-ordination and muscle movement. But he'd barely acknowledged the existence of the lamp or the toys. And he rarely sat in that corner.

When I drove into Ballater and picked Fraser up an hour or so later, I'd actually forgotten about the cord. He didn't mention it either.

It was only when I was talking to Chris that night that the subject came up again. A look of sheer horror flashed briefly across Chris's face when I told him about my discovery. But he too worked out that Fraser wouldn't have gone to school without knowing where it was. As we tucked him up in bed that evening, we both saw that the cord was lying exactly where it had been that morning, on the sideboard.

We went to bed that night puzzled but not overly worried. This was Fraser-world, after all. We'd long ago learned to expect the unexpected.

We would often go into Fraser's room in the morning to find the cord lying on his pillow, on the bedspread or, sometimes, on the floor, after he'd been playing with it late into the night. The next day, however, it remained untouched in the same position on the sideboard. And it was there the next morning too.

It was only that weekend that Chris and I began to realise that he must have turned some kind of corner.

'I wonder what's made him lose interest in the cord?' Chris said over our regular curry on the Saturday night.

'Well they said it was an anxiety thing, so maybe he's not so anxious at the moment,' I said.

'Isn't he? That's not what the therapists say is it?', Chris said.

It was true. Fraser had been attending the private nursery school now for the best part of ten months, since October 2010. His therapists had recommended some kind of nursery to help his communication and social interaction. State schools were out of the question, mainly because they wouldn't accept him until he was three and a half. We tried to get some help from the council to get funding for a private school but had hit a brick wall and had to find the money ourselves. We'd found a great nursery in Ballater and it was agreed that he would attend for the minimum allowed, two days a week. Chris and I paid for one day and Chris's parents had kindly offered to pay for the other. The staff at the nursery had really taken him to their heart and, whilst there were lots of problems, as there always were with Fraser, it was working out very well for us. Not least because it gave me a few hours off a couple of days a week.

Of course, we couldn't claim that Fraser had fitted in completely. His last report, a few weeks before Billy arrived, had been from the speech and language therapist, Marie. She had been to see Fraser at school and noted that he was making good progress in his use of language although it was still consistent with autism. While he'd started using what she called 'lovely sentences' he wasn't using simple words like yes and no. It was something I was more than familiar with, of course.

More worryingly, she said that he was still 'distant and isolated' from the other children at school and was happiest 'when he was not with other children'. The familiar behaviour from home was also present in the classroom where, the therapist said, Fraser 'continues to rock and sway when excited and covers his ears with his hands at times'.

All this suggested that Chris was right. There was no reason why he would suddenly discard his cord. He still needed to 'zone out' and escape when he came out from school.

We both sat there, lost in our thoughts for a

moment. There was nothing unusual there, especially when it came to Fraser. He had always given us plenty to think about.

'He might just have outgrown it,' Chris said after a while.

'Maybe,' I said.

'Let's think about it logically. What else has changed in the past few months?'

The silence that followed was interrupted by the clattering sound of the cat flap in the porch. We both knew immediately who it was.

We both looked at each other and shook our heads, almost simultaneously.

'No,' Chris smiled at me, getting up and heading for the porch to let Billy into the house after a couple of hours roaming the grounds in the fading light.

'It can't just be him. Can it?'

Chris could be as cautious and logical as he liked, as far as I was concerned there was no longer any denying that Billy had made an impact on the house in general and on Fraser in particular. The evidence was now too much to ignore.

Billy's arrival had coincided with a particularly busy time for us as a family. Looking after Fraser was a 24/7 job and Pippa was growing up fast too. She was an absolute joy and made me laugh a lot. She used to spend a lot of time in her favourite rocking chair and would often fall asleep in it with one leg slung over the side and an arm behind her, as if she was posing for *Vogue* magazine or something. I had also started taking her to a local toddler group where she was fascinated by the other children.

I also had the small matter of a house move to organise. Yet, somehow, this was all happening in an orderly, not-too-stressful way. There was no way that would have happened a year or two earlier.

The fact that Billy was such a calming and positive influence on Fraser was playing a part in creating this atmosphere, I was convinced. Sometimes it was simply the fact that he was around to distract and interact with Fraser. At other, more highly-charged times, his presence seemed to take a little of the anger out of Fraser. His meltdowns were slowly becoming six out of tens rather than full-blown nine or tens.

Whether Billy was having a deeper impact than this on Fraser was a question too far. But it wasn't just me who was recognising the impact he was having.

A few days before we were due to move my mum travelled up from Essex to stay for a week to help me with the final packing and to help with the children during the mayhem that was about to unfold. One particular morning she and I were sharing a cup of coffee. It felt like a well-deserved reward. We had been through our usual morning routine. As was the norm, Chris had got up and given Fraser his cereal and given him his toast and marmite cut into little squares the way he liked it. He had then eaten his yoghurt and his weak orange juice. He'd then had his face and hands wiped and his bib put away, as he liked it. It was something we'd evolved through those 'trial and horror' stages.

It was one of the days when Fraser wasn't at nursery, so he was with us, watching television and playing on the carpet as usual. He was thoroughly content.

My mum was sitting on her favourite chair in the living room, a slightly higher and wider chair than the low-slung leather sofa that I preferred. Billy was in the room, milling around, but everything was calm. That all changed in an instant when Billy decided, for no obvious reason, that he wanted to sit on my mum's lap.

Now the thing you need to understand is that my mum had been very wary of cats since an incident when she'd been pregnant with me. Apparently a cat had landed on her huge, dome-shaped tummy one day, scaring the living daylights out of her. She'd steadfastly refused to have a cat even sit on her lap ever since. So when Billy approached her and suddenly sprang into the air, his paws aimed at her lap, the results were predictable. Well, to begin with, at least.

It was a scene that is still etched in my mind. One moment my mum was sitting there in her pyjamas, cradling a coffee, the next Billy landed on her, plonking one paw on her leg and the other inside her coffee cup.

My mum just screeched. The cup went up in the air, sending scalding hot coffee everywhere.

For a moment, all was chaos. My mum was in a tizzy, wiping everything down. I was up on my feet, fretting over where the coffee had gone and whether anyone had been scalded by it.

It was Fraser's reaction that I remember most vividly, however. He had been sitting at the other side of the room, so had been a safe distance from the flying coffee. I wasn't sure quite how he was going to react but he suddenly let out the most enormous laugh.

Fraser called my mum Cokey because she always sang that old East End favourite, the Okey Cokey to him.

'Billy's in Cokey's coffee,' he said.

I exchanged a look with my mum and we both immediately burst out laughing.

'That's right Fraser,' I said.

'Yes, Billy's in Cokey's coffee,' he said again, by now laughing even louder.

Only Billy was immune to the infectious laughter that was spreading around the room. You would have expected him to flee with his tail between his legs but he hadn't, far from it. He'd simply retreated to a corner where he was scrupulously licking himself clean of the coffee.

'That's the beauty of having a pet around the house I guess,' she said, wiping herself down with a damp cloth in the kitchen as I cleared away the teacups.

'What do you mean, mum?' I said.

'Well, they can be a nuisance, but they can't half put a smile on even the most miserable face.'

She was so right. Two years, even twelve months earlier, ours had been a tense and tetchy household. We were always on edge, waiting for the latest, inevitable meltdown and constantly dealing with the latest developments in the saga that was Fraser's medical and educational life. It was utterly exhausting. There were times when Fraser sucked every single ounce of energy and life out of me. I'm sure I did laugh during that period. I'm not that humourless! But I don't remember the mood being particularly light-hearted or jolly in our house very often.

Maybe it was my mind playing tricks on me but, as I thought about it that morning, it occurred to me that since Billy had arrived there had been half a dozen moments when Chris and I had smiled or chuckled either at him or something relating to him.

Only a day or two earlier in the garden, for instance, Chris and I had been sitting there and had spotted him seemingly stranded halfway up a tree. We'd both had images of us calling the fire brigade to rescue him but before we knew it he'd leapt off a branch and, somehow, landed safely on the roof of one of the outhouses.

'How the heck did he manage that?' Chris said, grinning widely.

And now, this morning, he'd put a broad smile on everyone's face, even my mum's.

I knew Chris would shake his head disapprovingly at me if I said it out loud, but he couldn't stop me thinking it.

There was something special, something magical about this cat. I was so glad he'd come into our lives.

Chapter 6

Pastures New

One day, in August 2011, a delivery lorry loaded up all our furniture and possessions and Chris and I fitted the children and the two cats in their baskets into our equally crammed car. Together we then made the six mile drive west from Ballater to the tiny hamlet of Easter Balmoral, on the edge of the Balmoral Estate. It was our fourth change of address in the space of three years, except this time it felt like we really had found a home in which Fraser and Pippa could spend the rest of their childhood.

All in all, the Estate had been fantastically generous and understanding of our problems with Fraser. We couldn't have asked more from an employer really. Whenever Chris had needed time off to visit the hospital or deal with the latest crisis, they'd been really understanding. When we'd asked about moving on to the Estate itself they'd again been supportive. The property they'd offered us was a three bedroom, two storey house in what, strictly speaking, was known as Easter Balmoral but was referred to by everyone on the Estate as 'the village'. The collection of around twenty or so houses, some modern but others dating back to the 19th century, was no more than a few hundred yards from the gate house where we'd lived three years earlier but, from the moment we finished unloading and put the kettle on for the first time, it felt it was a family home. I couldn't see us moving again for a long time.

The house was modern and warm and the children had a nice bedroom each. There was also a little, enclosed lawn area with a low, picket fence around it. Ours was one of a half dozen or so cottages so there were even other families with small children in the neighbouring homes. It was an idyllic spot for children to grow up. There was tons of space for them to run free and ride their bicycles, there was even a little burn, or river, alongside the little road that ran by the back door. And, of course, there were the grounds of the Balmoral Estate itself to roam and explore.

Walking the grounds wasn't an option during our first few weeks on the Estate, however. We had actually moved at the busiest time of the year, the period when the Queen was in residence, as she always was during August and September. During the rest of the year, the grounds were open to the public with guided tours of the castle. The atmosphere was very relaxed and there were always busloads of tourists from all over the world, roaming the grounds quite freely. But everything was strictly off limits when the Queen was in residence. At almost every corner, it seemed, there were blacked out Range Rovers, Police and lots of men with walkie-talkies. We had a side entrance to our house but even we were asked to provide ID as we came and went.

It also meant that Chris was kept a lot busier dealing with members of the Court who had moved up from London. He always said that the atmosphere during the two months the Queen was in residence was totally different. During the rest of the year he pretty much had the place to himself and spent his time fitting new appliances and equipment or repairing and renewing the electrics. But when the Court was around he was constantly at their beck and call.

'Part of the job,' he'd say with a philosophical shrug of his shoulders at the end of another marathon day fixing fax machines or rewiring a makeshift office for a member of the Royal household.

It was a bizarre little world, in many ways. We were living in a sort of bubble. Around Balmoral and

Ballater, no one batted an eyelid when we said that Chris worked for the Queen and we lived on the Estate. A lot of people locally had connections to the Royal Family. They were one of the biggest employers in the area with links to local families that went back more than a century. A lot of the shops in Ballater had been given Royal Warrants over the years. The Royals were thought of as part of the community, members of the Deeside family.

But the moment we travelled away from Scotland, it changed. Whenever we visited England, friends and family were always fascinated by the life we led and always asked Chris for little bits of gossip. Of course, Chris being Chris, he always pretended there wasn't any. It wasn't that he didn't have tales to tell, because he did, lots of them, some of them very funny. He was just too professional and responsible to go broadcasting them.

A lot of people assumed that I must also have lots of stories. I often talked about how much I loved walking the grounds of the Estate, so I think they imagined that I bumped into the Queen or the Duke of Edinburgh every morning for a chat. The truth of the matter was that I had no real contact with the Family at all aside from attending the odd private party that they gave for staff every now and again.

Everyone settled into life in the new house pretty well. Chris certainly appreciated the extra few minutes he got in bed in the morning. He could get to work in a matter of minutes which, particularly during the dark, winter months, was a godsend. Pippa too was very content and had instantly settled into her new bedroom, where she was surrounded by all her favourite toys. She was now nine months old and was still in her cot where she would happily lie watching her favourite mobile while gurgling and laughing away to herself.

It was Fraser who faced the biggest challenges, as usual. For the first time, he had a bedroom upstairs which immediately posed him problems. He had made really good progress walking with his splints but he still couldn't walk up a flight of stairs. He simply didn't have the strength in his joints. So if Chris or I weren't around to carry him he would crawl up. He would then come down on his bottom, bump, bump, bumping his way, one step at a time.

This particular problem was on my list of things to tackle once we'd settled in. Chris had already had a word with a carpenter from the Estate about fitting some special handrails at Fraser's height to help him get in and around the house and, in particular, to climb the stairs. But there were so many other issues that still needed dealing with that it didn't seem a priority at that stage.

The first challenge was to get Fraser used to the new, slightly different atmosphere here. Life was a little busier on the Estate, even during the ten months of the year when the Queen wasn't in residence. Given Fraser's aversion to strangers, I knew that was going to present a few problems. At least they weren't unfamiliar ones.

When we'd lived at the gate house he had been really sensitive to people who poked their head into his buggy when we were walking around the grounds. They were, of course, being complementary and usually cooed over him. He was a pretty little boy.

But he really didn't appreciate the intrusions and could go absolutely crazy. He would refuse to look at or engage with the person and would start shouting and screaming, often at full volume. When he'd been a little baby it hadn't been so noticeable. All new babies cry. But as he'd got older it had been more and more embarrassing and difficult to deal with. On several occasions, I'd had to apologise to some poor, unsuspecting tourist and run off as fast as I could back home so that Fraser could cool down.

He was a little better now, but it was still an issue with him. So I was still careful to pick and choose my moments to take him and Pippa out for a walk and I generally avoided the peak tourist times.

The other issue he had was with people visiting the house. This had long been a problem with Fraser. If a delivery driver knocked on the door to deliver a parcel, for instance, he would get upset the moment he heard the doorbell. More often than not he'd end up halfway between the front door and the lounge, crying with his hands over his ears because he was afraid some strange person was going to come in and do God knows what to him.

So I always had to reassure him that no one was coming in and that it was going to be fine. It could be tricky, a little bit like Catch 22. If he was really upset he didn't want to stay in the front room or kitchen on his own, he wanted to stay with me. But if I had to open the door that meant he had to come with me, which meant that he could see the person at the door and get even more upset if he didn't like the look of them.

Talking to his therapists about it, we reckoned it was related to the atmosphere in the house. When someone else came in they changed the atmosphere and this could really affect Fraser. His mood would change after any visits and he would become very quiet and withdrawn. It affected him for hours and he could be difficult with me. So I had to be on top of it as much as possible and was careful to give him warning of any visitors as much as I could.

To be fair, Fraser had improved a little bit in the past 18 months or so because he'd got used to his therapists coming to visit us. Pippa had also had lots of visits from the health visitor. But he could still get very upset by a surprise visitor or anything that disrupted his routine. In the previous properties, especially in the house near Ballater and the cottage in the woods, they had been few and far between. But when we arrived on the Estate suddenly we did have more frequent visits, either from neighbours or members of the Estate staff.

That was the bad news. The good news, of course, was that we now had Billy to calm him down.

As we settled into life on the Balmoral Estate, no one was happier than Billy. The old house near Ballater had been set on relatively flat land, not far from the river. There had been trees but precious little else to explore. Balmoral itself was another story, of course. It was set in a spectacular landscape with wild, heather-filled moors, river valleys and forests to explore.

He still loved playing in the trees too, of course. One day Fraser was playing on a trampoline that we'd got him for the garden. He couldn't bounce up and down on it very much because of the weakness in his legs so he tended to just stand on the trampoline, gently rising and falling on the rubber mat in the middle while he held himself on the support bar.

He was standing there when he suddenly smiled and pointed upwards.

'There's my cat,' he said.

I looked up and got the fright of my life. Billy was

clambering up a tree and not any old tree, a massive one. He was soon what looked like fifty feet up in the swaying branches.

'Oh my God, Billy, what the heck are you doing?' I said out loud.

For a minute or so I was rooted to the spot, having palpitations about how he was going to escape. My imagination began to run wild and I saw him falling on to the road or, even worse, into the river and being swept away in full view of Fraser. But, of course, that was me being paranoid – and silly. Billy was in his absolute element. He couldn't have been happier, perched on a branch, looking down on Fraser as if he was guarding him. And there was no need for me to call the fire brigade. After a while he nonchalantly scampered down the trunk before leaping, what must have been 15 to 20 feet, on to the roof of the little woodshed that we had allocated to us on the edge of the river.

My heart stopped for a split second while he floated through the air. 'That cat is going to be the death of me,' I said to myself.

The Balmoral landscape offered pastures new for all of us, but for Billy in particular there was a whole new world to explore. And explore it he did. During the first couple of weeks he appeared a couple of times in the porch covered with what looked like miniature pine cones embedded in his coat. He must have been roaming the forests that skirted the Estate. Often he'd be gone for hours, yet we – and more importantly Fraser – rarely felt his absence.

What was amazing was that Billy could be goodness knows where doing goodness knows what but he somehow knew when he was on and off duty. So, for instance, I wouldn't see hide nor hair of him during the two days when Fraser was at nursery in Ballater. He would be around first thing in the morning, when Fraser could get a little agitated getting ready. But we wouldn't really see him again until Fraser got home. He seemed to know when we were due back and, several times, we had found him standing by the back gate waiting for us as we pulled up in the car. That always put a big grin on Fraser's face.

'My Billy's waiting for me,' he'd say.

He was usually around for Fraser's bedtime as well. He had learned that his presence was a huge reassurance for Fraser and would lay there at the bottom of the bed until he had nodded off to sleep. Occasionally he'd stay there all night but more often than not he would pad down the stairs and either go to bed himself or head out through the cat flap into the night. He had always returned home before Chris and I went to bed, however. Again, he seemed to know when the door to the outside porch was being locked and made sure he was inside in time.

What was most impressive was the sixth sense he seemed to have developed about Fraser. He somehow knew when Fraser was agitated or upset and would appear, as if by magic, at our times of need. One evening, a short time after we arrived at Balmoral, was typical.

Bathing Fraser had been a problem since he was a baby. He didn't like being immersed in water in general, especially if it was hot.

I have a picture of his first bath and you would think that he had been placed in a boiling hot bath. He was completely red but it wasn't from the heat, it was from screaming.

If giving him a dip in the bath was hard work, washing his hair was even worse. It was absolutely horrendous. He hated it more than he hated anything in the world and, in Fraser's case, that was saying rather a lot.

It became so bad that I couldn't face it, especially at the end of a long day. Chris would always give me a hand but even he couldn't bring himself to go through the experience more than once a week. I knew he should have a bath more often than that and felt certain there were mothers out there who would have judged me if they'd known. But I didn't care to be honest. If their child's bath-time had been such an abysmal experience, they'd have done absolutely the same thing.

In the 18 months or so following his official diagnosis, things had got a tiny bit better thanks to a plastic seat we'd been given to provide Fraser with extra support in the bath. It was the same issue again – pressure. Part of the drama at bath-time was down to the fact that Fraser was never happy being held back and dipped in the water. He didn't feel completely secure and there was no way he'd support himself in a bath; he simply wouldn't sit up on his own. This meant that Chris or I – or sometimes both of us – would have to hold him while we washed him. The plastic seat changed all that. Once Fraser had that support around him and he knew he wasn't going anywhere he was a lot happier. Until we suggested washing his hair, of course. Then all hell would usually break loose.

It was the same story as with his other outbursts. Once he went over to what I call the 'dark place' it was very hard to bring him back. So if we said in advance of pre-bed bath-time that we were going to wash his hair, it could result in him screaming and crying and lying on the floor absolutely rigid with fear. Even if we then abandoned the plans, we still wouldn't be able to get his bedtime clothes on. Sometimes we couldn't even get him calm enough to get into bed. The issue could trigger three hours of stress for all of us. So we'd learned to separate bath-time from washing his hair, with limited success.

One night, soon after we arrived at Easter Balmoral, Chris and I had braced ourselves for the weekly ordeal. We'd managed to get Fraser into the bath but pandemonium had broken out for some reason. He had turned bright red and was screaming 'no, no, no' and 'don't touch my hair' and covering his head with his hands. Chris and I knew the signs well enough. It was so bad that we were facing a real mother of all meltdowns, an eleven out of ten.

'This is pointless,' Chris said, exasperated after five minutes of bedlam during which we'd done little but avoid getting soaked as Fraser thrashed around with his hands. 'We aren't going to get anywhere tonight, I think we might as well get him out.'

I was inclined to agree. Apart from anything else, I thought our new neighbours might call the police because it must have sounded as if we were murdering a child. It was upsetting Pippa too, which was worrying given how easy-going she was generally. I was about to reach for Fraser's towel and start getting him out when I sensed an unexpected presence in the bathroom. Billy.

'What are you doing in here?' Chris said, as surprised as me to see him. To my knowledge, he'd never been in the bathroom before, either here or at the old house in Ballater.

He wasn't concerned about what we thought, it was obvious. He just wanted to hook up with his pal Fraser and was soon positioning himself at the side of the bath. Chris and I were still holding a flailing Fraser in the water but we slid over a little to give Billy some space. We then watched in mild disbelief as he lifted himself up and proceeded to put both paws on the edge of the bath. He then stretched himself up to his full height and leaned over as far as he could over the water so that he could push his face as close as he could to Fraser.

At this point Fraser was still agitated. But, as usual, Billy wasn't deterred by the histrionics. He did precisely what he would have done if we'd been downstairs, quietly positioning himself next to Fraser, and stayed there.

He was soon soaked to the skin. At one point Fraser flicked some of the bubble bath in his face and he had to wipe it away with his paw. But Billy remained fixed to the spot until Fraser started to calm down which, eventually, he did.

'Look Billy doesn't mind getting his hair wet, so why don't you let me wet yours?' Chris said, sensing an opportunity.

Fraser didn't say anything, which, for us at least, was tantamount to a yes.

Chris gently rubbed some shampoo into Fraser's head and worked it into a lather as I, quietly, got a small, plastic jug ready to rinse it out.

This was the bit that Fraser hated the most. He was terrified of showers so we used the jug instead but even this was a challenge, so we were braced for more fireworks. Billy remained in position, however, offering quiet reassurance.

I started washing the shampoo out with the jug. Ordinarily, it would have meant the outbreak of World War Three. But on this occasion he just let me gently wash out the soap. In fact, he went one step further and leant his head back to help the process.

If I'd been a more religious person I'd have considered singing Hallelujah.

'There, we're done, that wasn't so bad was it Fraser?' Chris said, a few moments later, a towel in his hand.

No sooner had we picked Fraser out and wrapped him up than Billy was padding his way off into Fraser's bedroom, ready for the next phase of the operation. He had been with us long enough to know that Fraser would take longer than usual to settle this evening. He must have sensed that his presence would make the difference between him nodding off to sleep within ten to fifteen minutes or an hour.

Ordinarily, I might have been miffed at the sight of wet paw prints across the landing and a rather soggy moggy lying on Fraser's duvet. But on this occasion I didn't mind one bit. I even brought an extra towel into the bedroom to give Billy a rubdown and a bit of a cuddle as well.

If anyone deserved it, he did.

'Where would we be without you?' I said, giving him an affectionate ruffle of the towel.

Chapter 7

Cutting Corners

One evening a couple of weeks after we'd moved to the 'village' I was sitting in the living room, flicking through the latest entries in Fraser's nursery diary when something caught my eye.

The staff had kept the diary since he'd begun, a year or so earlier, partly to keep us up-to-date with what he was getting up to each day but also to let us know about any progress he'd made. With all the upheaval of moving and settling into our new house, I'd not had a chance to take more than a cursory look at it for a few weeks.

The entry that jumped out at me had been made the previous week, in mid-August, around the time we'd moved. One of the assistants had recorded that

Fraser had 'drunk from an open topped cup'.

I was amazed. Drinking from an open topped cup might not have been a big deal to many mums but to me it was enough to make me sit up in my chair. Cups were a huge bone of contention with Fraser and always had been. He was incredibly picky not just about the colour and design of them but also how he drank out of them. It stemmed from his hypotonia, which meant he had difficulty holding anything. When he had begun holding cups to drink, he had done so unsteadily and with two hands clamped to each side. To make sure he didn't spill any, I'd added a cover with a spout. He'd become attached to this and had since steadfastly refused to drink out of anything that didn't have a spout on it. Well, until now, it seemed.

That's interesting, I thought to myself, making a note in the space for parents' comments.

Intrigued, I skimmed backwards to see what else I might have missed amid all the hullabaloo recently. Reading through the earlier entries, it was clear he was having a fun time at nursery; there were notes on how he had joined in a singing circle, helped in the garden and even gone on a short walk, which was something of a surprise to me.

But it was another note that really leapt off the page. It was dated June 28th, the day after Billy had arrived.

'Fraser washed his hands independently after coming in from play,' it read.

This one really stopped me in my tracks.

Fraser had a lot of idiosyncrasies that the nursery had got used to and his unwillingness to wash his hands was one of them. Ever since he'd joined, the classroom assistants had known to use 'wet wipes' to clean him when he covered himself in paint or anything else messy. If he really had learned to wash his hands himself, then this was a second, significant breakthrough.

Chris had had a long, busy day and was watching the news on television.

'Chris, there's something going on with Fraser at nursery,' I said, provoking an immediate twitch of an eyebrow.

'What sort of something?'

'Don't worry, it's not a problem, it's the opposite actually,' I added. 'Look at the entries I've marked,' I said, passing the book over.

'Hmmm. Interesting how he's just started to do those things on his own,' he said. 'But that's what he does isn't it? He does things when he's ready to do them.'

'But did you look at the date of the first entry?' I said.

'What about it?' he said.

'It's the day after Billy arrived.'

He gave me another one of those mildly disapproving looks that were becoming familiar now.

'That's just a coincidence Louise. It must be something they are doing with him at nursery. He didn't decide to wash his hands for the first time just because he got a new cat.'

I bit my tongue. There was no way in the world I could even begin to prove it, let alone explain it. But every instinct in my body told me there was a connection.

Fraser wasn't due in to the nursery again for a couple of days but I resolved to have a chat with Cath, the headmistress, to see if she'd noticed any change in him in recent weeks.

Cath had been incredibly supportive. In fact, without her, I don't know what we would have done with Fraser, education-wise.

In the dark days when Fraser was first diagnosed, we weren't quite sure where he was going to be educated. Given his diagnosis, we were advised that the most suitable place for him was a school in Aboyne which had what was referred to as a 'base unit' for children with behavioural, psychological and physical problems or disabilities. As Fraser had approached the age where he could begin nursery, we had visited it. We'd had no issue with the school; it seemed quite well-equipped. But we simply didn't think it was right for Fraser. To begin with, it would have meant a 16 mile drive to school and back, an hour or more in the car each day. More importantly the unit seemed, to me at least, to be too quiet for him. He needed stimulation and a lot of activity around him. The problem was that there were no other schools with specific facilities for autistic children. For a brief time we considered moving to be nearer to the town of Stonehaven where they had a special needs secondary school, the only one of its kind in the north of Scotland.

But it didn't make sense to go through that kind of upheaval. Chris would probably have had to find a new job and we would have had to buy a new house. It was too much.

By a twist of fate, Fraser wasn't going to start school until he was five and a half. The cut off for entry to a new school intake was February 28th and, thanks to my long labour, he had been born a day later, on March 1st. So we effectively had an extra year to work out what to do with his state education. In the meantime, however, we had to find him a nursery.

Chris and I visited all sorts of schools, some of which were private. To our delight, we found the best of them in Ballater.

It wasn't just that it was so close to where we lived at the time; the school also 'got' Fraser. This was in no small measure down to Cath, who had arrived a short time after Fraser started.

She had a son who had been diagnosed with autism at around five but was now fifteen. I told her a little about Fraser and his funny little ways, many of which rang true to her. Fraser loved naming the colour of cars that passed us by when we were out on the road, for instance.

'My boy did that. Soon Fraser will be naming the make of the car as well,' she told me. That had already come true.

The fact that she had so much experience of dealing with autism meant that she could pre-empt some of the issues for Fraser. For instance, she knew that he was liable to cut himself off from other children so had made a 'quiet corner' in the nursery where he could go if he was feeling overwhelmed. She had placed books and spinning toys there. Fraser had found it a great escape and often used it.

When I went to see Cath a couple of days after reading the diary entries she smiled.

'We were all really pleased. For some reason, he had been doing some messy play in the garden and came in to class and just headed for the taps,' she said of the hand washing.

'Really?' I said, slightly incredulous that he'd been

able to turn the taps on. I didn't think he had the strength because of his muscle tone and the weakness it had caused.

'He grabbed some soap and washed his hands, and then dried them,' she said. 'He's also stopped going into the quiet corner so much,' she said. 'In fact, I haven't seen him sitting there for weeks.'

'When did that start?' I said.

'About six weeks ago, around the same time he started washing his hands actually,' she replied.

I couldn't resist asking.

'Does he ever mention his cat?' I said.

'Billy?' Cath said. 'Oh my goodness, he talks about him all the time. "Billy climbed the tree." "Billy landed in grandma's coffee." "Billy is naughty." He's forever telling us about what he's been up to, we're all fascinated by Billy,' she smiled.

That was it for me. That was all the confirmation I needed. I knew no one else was likely to agree with me but, whatever the explanation, I headed home feeling elated. Something was happening and it was something very positive.

Fraser, Chris and I weren't the only ones to benefit from Billy, of course. The new air of calm that he had brought to the house also helped me with Pippa, who was growing up fast.

Pippa was so different to Fraser in so many ways but her birth had been almost as dramatic.

We had been delighted when I fell pregnant again in the spring of 2010. At the back of our minds there was inevitably that question mark: would we have another autistic child? Apparently, if you have had one, the chances of you having another are significantly higher, as much as 1 in 20 according to some. Ordinarily the chances are 1 in 5,000.

So we'd elected to have a private scan when I was 22 weeks to see what sex the baby was. If we were going to have another boy then we would have to be prepared for him to be autistic because autism is much more common in boys than girls. We weren't afraid of that; we simply wanted to be as ready as we could be, especially given what we'd been through with Fraser.

Chris and I had travelled to Aberdeen prepared for all eventualities. As it turned out, we found out we were having a girl, which had delighted us both. The idea of having a boy and a girl was lovely but it also reduced the risk significantly.

I'd talked it through with the doctors and, because of the problems I'd had with Fraser, I'd elected to have a C-section. It was all planned for November 24th 2010 but I had really bad pre-eclampsia, even worse than when I was pregnant with Fraser, which complicated matters. Adding to my woes, it took the medical team six attempts to administer the epidural. So what should have been a relatively straightforward delivery became a drama. Again.

After the birth they nearly lost me, apparently. One moment I was holding and cuddling Pippa, the next I was vomiting and having fits. My blood pressure had shot up to such an extent that an emergency team arrived with one of those CPR trolleys you see in *ER*.

I remember asking one of the nurses, 'Am I going to be all right?'

'I don't know,' she'd replied, which would have been a cause for concern if I'd remained conscious, but I didn't.

I was soon looking like a pin cushion as they injected me and hooked me up to various drugs. Poor Chris had to stand there watching it all while he held on to Pippa.

Of course, Fraser being Fraser, he was at the centre of a drama of his own when his sister was born. My mum had come up to look after him and was on her own in the house outside Ballater. On the day of my C-section, she answered the front door in the porch to a delivery man, leaving the front door to the house open. Fraser had become upset by the delivery man and shut the door, locking her out. To make matters worse, the winter snow had decided to arrive that day and there was already six inches of white stuff outside. My mum had been left standing there in her slippers in the middle of a blizzard. All the other doors and windows were locked and she'd got herself into a terrible state.

By a complete fluke another van drove past the house. She flagged it down and got the guy to kick down the door. The only consolation was that Fraser had been sitting in the living room, watching television, completely oblivious to the unfolding drama.

When Chris had rung with the news of Pippa's birth, my mum had barely been back in the house for ten minutes and was still recovering from the ordeal.

'She didn't sound very excited,' he'd said to me back in the delivery suite.

It was only when we got home that we discovered why.

One of our biggest concerns in the run up to Pippa's birth was that Fraser wouldn't like his little sister. But that was quickly dispelled.

When I was eventually released, just in time to get back before the snow really set in, Fraser had been pretty disinterested to be honest. He seemed genuinely pleased to see me because it was the first time we'd been separated – which was rather lovely because at that point he rarely showed emotion – but he was his normal self with Pippa. He came to take a look at her in her cot but wandered off after a couple of minutes.

The feeling was pretty mutual. Pippa was so quiet and easy-going she even slept through Fraser's meltdowns.

To me, Pippa was a gift. The contrast with Fraser was total. She barely cried, in fact she was so quiet we worried about that fact she made no sound at all. When she wanted feeding or her nappy changing she let out what I'd call a whimper. Compared to Fraser's bellowing and screaming, it was heaven.

But I knew she needed care and attention as well, and I often bemoaned the fact that Fraser demanded so much of my time.

There was no doubt that Billy had freed up some of my time for Pippa. When I sat and reflected on it, I could see that he was helping us in so many ways.

The breakthroughs at the nursery set a new wave of determination coursing through me. 'Strike while the iron is hot, Louise,' I said to myself. And so I did.

The issue I was really sick to death with at that particular time had been a bone of contention for years – Fraser's dummy.

There was, of course, nothing particularly unusual

about a young child being fixated on their dummy, or soother as they are more popularly called these days. What was unusual was the length of time that Fraser had remained obsessed by it and the way he had become preoccupied with the exact type of dummy that he had. It was a simple one made by Tommee Tippee. Woe betide me if I didn't have the right one or – even worse – tried to take it out of his mouth.

It was something that had bugged me for a long time now. Aside from everything else, it was embarrassing. He had been using it at nursery from the very beginning and was still prone to sticking it in his mouth when he felt stressed. They were understanding but that wasn't always the case around Ballater.

The previous year, for instance, it had caused a horrible incident when we were shopping.

Going shopping with Fraser had never been easy. Even going into the small Co-op in Ballater was a major issue and we used to avoid it as much as we could.

The shop was tiny and everything was squeezed into such a small space, which made it very difficult to get a buggy round the aisles. Fraser found it very claustrophobic so almost always cried. As it happened, on this particular day he hadn't cried, partly because had his dummy in. I had been feeling quite pleased that we were going to get in and out without a drama when an old man came past us tutting. That wasn't so unusual, I got a lot of tuts and frowns when I was out with Fraser. People thought he was too old to be in a buggy, too old to have a dummy, too old to be crying so much. If I had a pound for every disapproving look I'd been given, I'd have been a rich woman. What happened next, however, was out of the ordinary. The old man had reached the till before us and had just finished paying for his shopping.

Without any warning whatsoever he turned round and said: 'You dannae need that, you dannae need a sook.' He then leant down and took the dummy out of Fraser's mouth. Just like that.

The lady on the till was gobsmacked. I was gobsmacked. What on earth was he thinking? For a split second, I froze. The man put the dummy on the counter and shuffled out the door. The lady at the till grabbed it and handed it back to me with an apologetic shrug of her shoulders but, of course, it was too late. The damage was done.

Fraser went absolutely ballistic. He just went from nought to ninety on the angry scale in about two seconds flat. His screams were soon drawing looks of utter disgust from the shoppers and I had to abandon my shopping and beat a hasty retreat back to the car where I had to spend ten minutes calming him down and reassuring him that the man didn't mean to upset him. It had really upset me and put me completely off shopping in Ballater for a while. It was why, when we now went shopping, Chris came along and stayed in the car with Fraser. I just couldn't cope with the dirty looks and the tutting.

That was bad enough. But the dummy problem had begun to reach a real crisis point a few weeks before we moved into the 'village' at Balmoral. One morning I had grabbed a new packet of dummies, taken one out and put it in Fraser's mouth.

No sooner had I done so than he had fired it out of his mouth like a cannonball being fired from a cannon. It just flew across the kitchen and on to the floor. He then began screaming.

'What on earth is that about?' I said to Chris, who was finishing off a cup of tea before heading in to work.

He just shrugged his shoulders and pulled a face as if to say 'not a clue'.

I had taken the dummy from a new box. Maybe there was something wrong with this batch, I thought. I knew there was an older box somewhere in the cupboards so took a dummy from there and put it in Fraser's mouth. Bizarrely that seemed to placate him.

I made myself a cup of tea and then sat down to compare the two dummies. At moments like this, I couldn't help dwelling on the ridiculousness of my life. Here I was, scrutinising the difference in baby's dummies as if I was an art dealer assessing an Old Master portrait. I felt silly and, even more ridiculously, I had no idea what I was looking for.

Hard as I tried, I couldn't see any differences whatsoever. But then as I was just about to give up, I noticed a small, almost imperceptible difference. There was an extra ridge on the teats.

'Oh my God, they've changed it,' I said to myself.

'They've changed the flippin' dummy and he's spotted the difference,' I said to Chris who must have thought he was living with a lunatic.

Chris looked at me in disbelief.

'How could he possibly know the difference?'

'I don't know Chris, but he has,' I said, as I hurriedly started looking in the cupboards as a new panic began to dawn.

'Oh no,' I said, realising that I only had one box of the old ones left.

This wasn't going to last more than a few days, a week at the most given the way Fraser rejected them regularly if he didn't like the look of them. I had to get hold of a supply of the old-style dummies. Fast.

That morning I started sending emails that, with their ridiculously specific language and occasional use of hysterical CAPITAL LETTERS, would have looked absolutely stark raving bonkers to any casual observer. Fortunately, the recipients knew they related to Fraser so they were no crazier than any of the emails I'd been sending over the past few years.

I had sent them to Chris's mum and my relatives

down in Essex asking them to scour every shop, internet site and other potential source they could think of for the old model of the Tommee Tippee dummy 'NOT the NEW and IMPROVED one!!!'

To their credit, they all agreed and – even better – were soon dispatching a steady flow of dummies up to us. But I had known this was only going to last a short time. The old dummies had been discontinued and the supplies would eventually run out. It had been a cloud hanging over us, a ticking time bomb counting down to the moment we ran out of the right dummies and the explosion that would inevitably follow.

We were, by my reckoning, a few weeks away from that moment now so I had decided to act. Given what had been happening at nursery and the improvements at home since Billy's arrival, I felt it was the right time to strike. Time was running out and, besides, I really had had a bellyful of the tutting and people looking at me as if to say 'you're a bad mother'.

And so it was that, on the day after talking to Cath about Fraser's progress, I resolved to do something which most people would probably think was extreme. I waited until mid-morning when Fraser had settled in the front room watching television. I opened the cupboard in the kitchen, took down the large, plastic container in which I kept the dummies and placed it on the table. I then took out the large kitchen scissors and began snipping the teats off them. It was weirdly cathartic. Snipping the first one felt good. Snipping the last felt even better.

When Fraser came into the kitchen for his usual, mid-morning drink with Billy in tow, I braced myself and delivered the line that I'd been preparing in my head all through the previous night.

'I'm really sorry, Fraser, but the dummies are broken,' I said, holding up one of them with the teat snipped off.

He looked at me quizzically. I could see the machinations were already going on in his head. As usual, I had no idea what they were and what reaction they were going to provoke.

I had steeled myself for him to scream the house down, but there was nothing but a silence that seemed to go on for minutes.

I daren't speak myself. I sensed that I needed Fraser to process this information if I was to have any chance of succeeding. After a few moments, he just shrugged his shoulders, turned to his friend Billy who was sitting on the kitchen floor and said: 'oh dear, the dummy's broken Billy.'

He then took his snack and a drink, spun on his heels and headed back into the living room. I didn't know whether to laugh or cry. I felt elated, as if I'd won a gold medal at the Olympics.

I knew that I had to build on this so I repeated the

process again in the evening. Again I produced a dummy with a missing teat top and again Fraser looked at it, frowned and walked away.

Within two days, he had stopped asking for his dummy. The reaction was so dramatic that we didn't even allow him to have one at night, which he'd done for years.

I actually cry now when I think back to that moment. It sounds silly, I know, but it was a huge deal for us.

And I was in no doubt about what the catalyst was. Chris could tut and raise his eyebrows as much as he liked. Billy had somehow changed things for Fraser. The evidence was irrefutable, you could have taken it to a court of law and won I reckoned. The world pre- and post-Billy were utterly different. Before he arrived, everything was an issue, everything was a drama. But once Billy arrived, everything stopped being an issue all the time. For years, it had been a battle to reach each and every milestone. Suddenly, we were reaching them easily and without any real drama.

It was crazy. This dummy situation was a prime example. Not that long ago I was stressed out searching the country for the right dummy. It had been the same with the red cord.

It was now clear to me that the props that Fraser needed for security were starting to fall away. His red cord, his dummy, slowly the things he had needed to stay safe and secure were now becoming surplus to requirements. And they were becoming surplus because he had something else – he had Billy.

I wasn't claiming that he had super powers or anything daft like that. Billy didn't go there and physically take the dummy away. But there was no question in my mind that somehow he was enabling Fraser to chill out and relax and to realise that everything wasn't a big deal. I have no idea how he was doing it, but he was doing it. And I couldn't have been more grateful for that.

Chapter 8
A.W.O.L.

It was late autumn 2011 but already the nights were lengthening and had the feel of winter about them. Tonight it was pitch black outside and, to judge from the way it was whistling like a banshee in the windows, there was a violent wind building.

'When was the last time you saw Billy?' Chris said as he locked the back door and flicked off the light in the washroom where Billy ordinarily slept.

'Not since this afternoon,' I said. 'He played a bit with Fraser when he got back from nursery but wasn't around this evening, which was odd come to think of it.'

'Hmmm. It's not like him to still be out at this time. Especially in this weather,' Chris said, checking the porch at the front of the house where Billy came in through the cat flap in the door.

We exchanged a look that we both understood immediately.

Chris flicked the washing room light back on, unlocked the back door and stuck his head out into the rear garden.

'Billy,' he shouted, to little avail. The sound of the wind roaring through the trees was drowning out everything.

'You go to bed Louise,' he said, grabbing a coat and a torch. 'I think I'll take a little look around.'

As he stepped out into the night, my head was immediately flooded with thoughts. None of them were good.

Billy was an enigma in lots of ways. On the one hand, he was this very loving, cuddly creature at home. But he was also a free spirit who loved roaming the countryside, especially here at Balmoral. Since moving here he'd been out a lot more than he had been at the previous house. It was obvious why; the Estate and its wildlife offered rich pickings. People conveniently forget that cats are essentially predators. It's in their DNA to go out and hunt other creatures. Billy almost certainly ate most of what he caught, but he had got into the habit of bringing bits of prey home.

In the months since we'd moved to Balmoral, he

had shown up with mice, moles and voles. Chris was pretty certain he was also after the baby rabbits that lived in the woods. The Estate keepers tended to shoot them as vermin so they were the easiest pickings of all.

The results of his hunting habit weren't very pleasant to behold.

Only the previous week he had arrived in the front porch with a little bird in his mouth. I'd been about to take the children to a toddler group at the local school in Crathie, a short distance from Balmoral, and was on the verge of stepping into the porch. Spotting him in there with this poor little bird, I ushered them into the utility room and out through the back door instead. Fraser wouldn't have understood what was happening and would almost certainly have been upset. I had called Chris and asked him if he could pop home and dispose of the evidence before we got back.

I, myself, had mixed feelings about cats and their predatory habits. Part of me thought they should be confined to quarters, as they are in some parts of the world, but part of me accepted it was simply the law of the jungle, or the Scottish moors and woodland in our case. At this precise moment, however, I had to admit animal ethics weren't high on my agenda. To be honest, I didn't care if he brought home a dead rat. I wanted him back in the house safe and well.

I knew there was no point me going to bed while Chris was out looking for him. I'd never fall asleep. So I flicked on the kettle and made myself a cup of cocoa. As I stood there, sipping my drink and staring into the blackness outside, the prospect of losing him was just too horrendous to think about.

Of course Billy was a major part of my worry. I'd grown so fond of him; I was seriously concerned about what had happened to him. But, if I was honest, I was most worried about how it would affect Fraser if Billy had gone missing. The two of them were so close; they had become inseparable soul mates. How on earth would I break it to him? How would he react? Could he actually handle it? Suddenly my mind was running at 100 mph but fortunately, at that moment, Chris reappeared. I could tell from his body language that he'd had no luck.

'Nothing?' I said.

'No,' he said with a shrug of his shoulders.

'I took a look around the garden and stuck my head in the woodshed. I've seen him sniffing around there before so I thought it was worth a try. It's too dark out there. We'll have to wait until the morning and hope he's turned up,' he said.

'But what will we do if he doesn't come back?' I said, trying not to let my voice crack.

'Let's just wait until the morning. I'm sure he'll turn up,' he said, giving me a hug, which was enough to trigger the waterworks. I felt so silly crying over a missing cat but I simply couldn't stop myself.

As was usual now because of Billy's hunting habits, we locked the door to the front porch so that he couldn't get into the house with a dead animal. If he came in through the cat flap on the outside door, he'd have to sleep in there. It was warm enough, even on a wild and windy night like tonight.

We trudged upstairs, saying very little, both knowing we were unlikely to sleep much as we waited for the telltale sound of the cat flap opening. Not that we were likely to hear it amidst the whistling and roaring of the winds that seemed to be growing stronger by the hour.

We both slept fitfully and Chris got up at least twice to check downstairs but there was no sign of him.

We were both up earlier than normal the next day. A thin, grey light was breaking to the east. There was still no sign of Billy.

Because of his increasing interest in the outdoors, we'd been priming Fraser in case he was ever away for longer than normal. We'd told him that Billy went out of the house and he accepted it. We had figured that, maybe, in his autistic brain, he treated it as one of those things that happened in life, like daddy going to work.

'He will be back home soon,' Chris said, repeating the same message again this morning.

I couldn't bring myself to look at Fraser. I had a horrible knot in my stomach. I just hoped that Chris was right.

Billy had gone out after dark before, but he had never gone completely A.W.O.L. and stayed out overnight. He had always come in before we locked up so I was seriously worried that something bad had happened to him.

Typically, I had already started beating myself up. *Why hadn't we kept him indoors or fitted him with a luminous collar?* I thought to myself. But I knew that would have been pointless. Those were things you did if you lived in a town or a city. We didn't live there, we lived in a remote and wild part of Scotland.

Inevitably, I had run through various theories about what had happened to him. Elsewhere in the country, cars were the biggest cause of accidental death but that wasn't really the case here. There were, to be honest, very few people on the roads even if Billy had wandered on to them, which was unlikely. It was far more likely that he had got himself injured or possibly attacked by another animal, although there weren't too many dangerous creatures here either. Balmoral was an important habitat and home to all sorts of creatures, from red deer and red squirrels to a whole range of birds, including red and black grouse and a very rare relative of theirs called the capercaillie. Few of them hunted cats, to my knowledge at least.

The more I thought about it, the more helpless I felt. So I decided to do something proactive at least. I couldn't just sit in the house and wait.

Fraser didn't have nursery that morning so, after clearing the breakfast stuff away, I decided to take him and Pippa for a walk around the grounds. By 9 a.m. the winds had died down and there were even a few slivers of pale blue in the sky. It looked like we might get a half decent day so I put them both in the double buggy and headed off. I had to do something and who knew, I might find Billy hanging out in someone else's house or playing with one of the other cats that I knew lived on the Estate.

As I set off on the road that ran through the Estate, I saw a couple of neighbours.

'I don't suppose you've seen our cat have you?' I asked one of them, trying to keep my voice down so that Fraser didn't get alarmed.

'The grey one who's always up the tree?' he said. 'No, I haven't but I'll keep an eye out for him.'

I wrapped my scarf up tight, buttoned down the cover on the children's buggy and headed off towards the main buildings of the Estate.

I loved walking around Balmoral. During the darker times, when I'd really been struggling with Fraser, it had been one of the few things that had kept me sane. It felt like such an escape to stick the children in their buggy and take a stroll, regardless of the season. The Estate and its woodland trails and gardens was as beautiful in winter as it was in summer, in fact walking the grounds when the snow was down was one of the highlights of the year. The air was so crisp and clean, you felt like every breath was doing you a power of good.

I pushed the buggy past the house that was built for Queen Victoria's favourite John Brown, where the head of the Estate, the Factor, now lived. It looked right over the golf course where the Royal Family sometimes played. It was too late in the year for anyone to be out so I scoured the greens and the bunkers for a sign of Billy. I knew he wouldn't be there, but I was getting more desperate by the minute. 'Where the hell are you Billy?' I kept muttering quietly to myself.

It's about a ten minute walk to the main part of the Estate, where the Castle stands. There were so many places that Billy could have escaped to it was ridiculous. It really was like looking for a needle in a haystack.

One of my favourite spots is Garden Cottage, where Queen Victoria used to like staying. It's a lovely, little stone building that sits on the lawns near a walled garden. Fraser had always loved it there, especially when I took him through a gate under a rose arch and into the garden to see the conservatory. I walked past the cottage and the conservatory today, hoping to see a flash of grey in the greenery, but I had no such luck.

I did the same in the three acre kitchen garden that the Duke of Edinburgh had created a few years earlier and where the Royal Family get their vegetables from when they are in residence. Again, there was no sign of Billy.

After about an hour, I'd covered a huge swathe of the Estate. We'd seen a couple of the gardeners and general maintenance guys along the way but we drew nothing but blanks.

I knew that the children would soon be complaining so I headed back towards the house. The knot that had formed in my stomach the previous night had tightened another couple of notches. I really was beginning to fear the worst now.

It was Fraser who saw him first.

'Billy's back Mummy,' he said, as we approached the first of the cottages on the edge of the Estate.

'Is he? Where?' I said.

'There. Look,' Fraser said jabbing a finger in the direction of the fence.

My eyesight wasn't as good as his, so it took me a

moment to spot him. But sure enough, there Billy was, standing on the fence near the front gate. It was as if he was waiting for us.

It sounds crazy but I felt the weight of the world lifting off my shoulders. I could quite easily have cried. But I didn't want the children to think there was anything untoward so I kept it together and simply sped up the buggy.

Billy was pretty bedraggled but there was no obvious sign of any wounds or scratches. In fact, he looked rather pleased with himself. As I approached the gate, he arched his back and gave us a look as if to say 'what's all the fuss?'

'You have no idea how worried I've been about you,' I felt like saying to him, but I didn't want to alarm the children.

'See, I told you he'd be back later this morning, Fraser,' I said instead.

Inside the house, I saw that Billy's coat was covered in what looked like hair curlers. I think they must have been thistles or miniature pine cones of some kind, which told me he'd probably strayed a fair way, maybe up towards the moors above the Castle. I knew there were dense, pine forests up there. Maybe he'd found shelter and decided to spend the night riding out the storm. Goodness knows what he'd been up to. I'd never know. But, to be honest, at this point I didn't much care.

After making the children a little snack I decided to give Billy a wash, which he didn't much like. Fraser joined in, hosing him down with the shower head and chastising Billy for not sitting still when he tried to wriggle free from the jet of water being directed at him, which struck me as pretty ironic.

He was delighted to be released into the towel I had waiting for him.

'Don't do that to us again, Billy,' I said under my breath as I ruffled his coat with a towel and let him jump out of my hands.

Of course I knew that, even if he could have understood me, there was zero chance of him listening.

Chapter 9

Stepping Stones

When people talk about 'man's best friend' they always refer to dogs. I understand why; I have known and loved lots of dogs myself. But, as Fraser's friendship with Billy developed, I began to see how unfair it is that cats don't get the same credit. Because it's clear they deserve it.

All I had to do each day was walk into my living room and see Fraser and Billy together to be convinced that the relationship between humans and cats could be pretty special too.

It beggared belief, to be honest. The bond they had formed was so much deeper and more profound than I could have anticipated. Yes, I'd hoped Billy would make a companion, a playmate. But he had become so much more than a fluffy ball of fun to roll around with on the carpet. He had the ability not just to get Fraser's attention but to hold it for hours at a time. Nothing had occupied his interest like that before. Not even a washing machine. There were times when they were locked in their own little world, sitting together while Fraser jabbered away often incoherently. It was almost as if they had a secret language.

Billy also gave Fraser so many other important things: loyalty, consistency, reassurance, encouragement and a sense of security. He was also, often quite literally, a shoulder for Fraser to lean on.

As the weeks and months went by, Billy was becoming our best friend too. Chris and I felt like we had a new partner in our day-to-day battle to deal with Fraser and his idiosyncrasies. As we settled into life in the new house, this gave me a new sense of confidence and strength. With Billy at my side, I sensed I might now be able to take on some battles that I'd felt too weak and vulnerable to face.

There had been so many of them that, at times, I had felt overwhelmed. Getting Fraser to walk properly. Getting Fraser potty trained. Getting Fraser to use a knife and fork properly. The list went on and on – and on. Before Billy, I'd felt incapable of tackling let alone winning far too many of them. I didn't feel that way anymore.

So in the weeks following my success with the dummy I decided to tackle another long-running problem – the stairs.

There was good reason to do this. As part of his ongoing physiotherapy, Fraser was going to be visited by someone who was going to assess his movement and motor abilities. He'd made great progress in other areas, thanks largely to Helen and the splints. They helped his balance and stability enormously.

But the stairs were still a problem area, partly because he'd never really had to negotiate them before. This was the first home in which he'd slept upstairs other than at Chris's parents' house. My mum and dad lived in a bungalow.

So, at the moment, Fraser was either crawling his way up to his bedroom or being carried up by me or Chris, which wasn't ideal for all sorts of reasons, not least the fact he was getting heavier by the day. I often felt breathless by the time I'd reached the top of the stairs if I had to carry him when Chris wasn't around.

With Helen no longer around, the new physiotherapist was a lady called Lindsey. She was due in December, about two weeks before Christmas, so in mid-November I decided it was time to step things up, so to speak.

The first thing we needed was to get the extra rails fitted so, after asking the Factor his permission to modify the house, we asked the Estate's joiner, Mike, over. He began by fitting a metal pole cum rail by the step outside. He then spent a day making a really nice rail inside. It was made of wood and was just the right size for small hands.

Almost immediately I started encouraging Fraser to use the new equipment. On days when he didn't have nursery, I would spend half an hour or so standing on the half-landing that breaks up the climb upstairs. There were about half a dozen steps leading to it.

'Let's see if you can use the rail to get up the stairs to me,' I would say.

I would then cheer and clap him as he made his way up the small flight of steps.

It was very hit and miss, naturally. Some days he would refuse point blank to even attempt to climb a single step. Others he would walk one or maybe two steps then crawl the rest. At other times he would lean against the wall and sort of slide upwards, using his hands to push off the steps. But every now and again he would raise up his hands, grab the rail firmly and pull himself up, step by step.

'Well done, Fraser,' I'd say every time he did.

I could tell it was going to take time and lots of practice, but I felt confident we'd get there.

The deep, concrete step outside the house was a more immediate success. When he came home from nursery or if we had been out shopping or to the doctors, I would ask him to use the rail to get himself up the single step. To begin with he would lean on the wall or place a hand on it to give him balance. But after no more than a dozen attempts, he was soon managing the step quite well while holding on to the handrail.

He seemed quite pleased with himself when I clapped him each time. Often he'd look for Billy, who was invariably at hand.

'Fraser climbed the step, Billy,' he would say.

I had forewarned him that a therapist was coming to see him and would ask him to walk up the stairs. So he was prepared when Lindsey arrived one brutally cold December morning.

I wrapped Fraser up warm for the outdoor part of the test. He struggled to do it without the rail and either held on to the wall or me until he felt steady. But when it came to walking using the rail, he passed with flying colours.

'Good, Fraser,' Lindsey said as he easily walked up holding on to the handrail.

He was pleased and gave me a big, beaming smile.

The stairs inside were less of a success. When Lindsey asked him to walk up and down without the rail he either leaned heavily on the wall or crawled up then bumped down on his bottom. On one occasion he did walk the last two steps, but only when Lindsey offered him a hand to help.

He fared a little better using the rail. He managed to climb up to the half landing by holding on to the rail with his left hand and placing his right hand on the step in front of him to steady himself. Despite Lindsey's encouragement, he bumped his way down every time.

She said she would write a report in the New Year and come back to see how he had progressed sometime in January.

'I'm sure he will have made a lot of progress by then,' she said.

Christmas came and went pretty quietly, as it generally did with us. For some reason, Fraser had never really engaged with it. Unlike most children, who would work themselves up into a frenzy by December 24th, he just carried on as normal.

This was going to be our fourth Christmas with him and I'd hoped things would change this year, but they hadn't. His nursery had put on a nativity play and there had been carols and a visit from Father Christmas. He had also been to the special party for the children of Balmoral staff where, along with every other little boy and girl, he'd been given a present from the Queen. He'd loved his present, a bear that would sing when you squeezed its tummy or hands, but even that hadn't really fired him up.

It upset me because, as a parent, it just reminded me of the fact that he was different. Perhaps selfishly, I'd dreamed of doing all the stuff that parents do – wrapping the presents, putting up the tree and decorations, leaving stuff out for Father Christmas on Christmas Eve. We did all those things but Fraser barely registered them. He treated Christmas Day pretty much like any other. He didn't like changing his routine too much.

Of course, it wasn't just about him. We had Pippa to worry about too. She was still too young to appreciate it, of course, but we had still got her lots of presents and she really seemed to like the Christmas tree and decorations.

It was a measure of how difficult Christmases had been for us that we had only spent one at home – and that was only because we'd been snowed in. We had spent one with Chris's mum and another down with my mum in Essex. But we weren't going to travel down there this year, partly because we couldn't face the eleven hour drive with Fraser but also because we were due to spend Christmas with Chris's mother this year. Also, at the back of my mind, I didn't want to separate Fraser and Billy for too long.

We had made a contingency plan for the cats. Our neighbours Sandy and Cilla had agreed to pop in to feed them and check they were OK. They had a little grandson, Murray, who loved cats so he was going to help them.

As we got ready to leave on Christmas morning, Fraser had been more concerned about laying everything out for Billy than he was with his presents.

He put out a bowl for his food and another dish for his water. He then spent ten minutes explaining to Billy that he was going to his grandma's house. He told him that Cilla and Sandy and Murray were going to pop in to see him.

'Murray will play with you,' he said, stroking him.

It was a little over the top given we were going to head back that night but it was worth it because it meant that Fraser's mind was at rest. He didn't worry about Billy during the journey or when we arrived at Chris's mum's place. He knew exactly what Billy was going to be doing and who was going to be seeing him so, in his autistic mind, all was well. Which was great.

As we settled back into the routine post-Hogmanay, as even I now called New Year, I got back to trying to help Fraser climb the stairs. The only difference now was that I had, without realising it, acquired an assistant.

One morning, early in January, I noticed that Billy had positioned himself on the half landing, in the identical spot where I'd been standing to encourage Fraser a couple of hours earlier.

I'd never noticed him sitting there before. If he ventured up the stairs for a snooze he tended to go all the way up to Fraser's bedroom – or stayed downstairs in the utility room or the living room. At first, I thought nothing of it.

The next day I was in the kitchen and I heard Fraser calling his name.

'Billy, Billy. Wait,' he said.

I walked out into the hallway to see Billy sitting, right on the edge of the half landing, overlooking the six steps below. Fraser was standing on the second step and was slowly walking up to meet him. It took a real effort on his part and once he got there he gave out a little puff, as if he was exhausted. He then lay down with Billy on the landing.

Again, I thought nothing of it. I just thought how sweet it was. When it started happening regularly I just put it down as a new phase of play they were going through. Even when I noticed that I was having to hoover the carpet on the half landing more often, to get rid of the matted cat hairs that Billy had left there, I didn't put two and two together.

It was only when I glimpsed them together one evening that the penny dropped.

I'd had another stair session with Fraser earlier during which he'd been less than co-operative, shall we say. He had walked up a couple of steps using the rail a few times but had quickly reverted to crawling. He hadn't even attempted to go down in an upright position. I knew when it wasn't worth the effort so I'd given up pretty quickly. Sometimes there was no point in pushing Fraser.

Billy had again positioned himself on the stairs, this time halfway up the steps leading to the half landing. Fraser had started walking up the steps towards him and was within touching distance. But then suddenly Billy reversed himself upwards on to the landing.

'Billy. Wait,' Fraser said, walking a little faster now as he chased him up the stairs. 'Wait.'

It was only when Fraser arrived on the half landing that Billy stopped moving. At that point he stuck his head straight in his pal's chest and started playing with him.

'Oh my goodness,' I said out loud.

I suddenly saw it. He was basically telling Fraser that, if he wanted to play with him, he had to climb the stairs to do it. What's more he had given him such an incentive to get to the top of the stairs that Fraser had moved as fast as he possibly could. I had never seen him move so fluidly and easily up the stairs.

I didn't know what to think. My head was suddenly spinning. He must have somehow picked up on my coaxing and cajoling on this same spot and – goodness knows how – decided to do the same thing. It seemed utterly impossible. Mad, actually. A little part of me actually thought I was losing a grip.

'Louise, come on,' I said as my mind raced at 100mph again.

Of course, Chris thought I'd been on the gin all afternoon when I mentioned it that evening. He was a huge believer in Billy and was the first to tell people what a calming influence he had become around the house. But he wouldn't accept that he did more than that. It was too far-fetched for him.

Of course, what I needed was for Billy to do it again. But sod's law came into play and they didn't repeat the process again that evening, or indeed any other evening while Chris was around. During the daytime they would regularly hang out on the landing, with Billy slowly backing up the stairs as Fraser tried to catch him. It was so frustrating; I even thought about filming it to prove to Chris that it really was happening.

But I knew what I'd seen. And I knew what it meant.

149

Early in January, we got a copy of the report that Lindsey had written after her visit in December. It said precisely what we thought it would say; that Fraser 'leaned heavily on the wall and often opted to crawl up the stairs' and that he 'bumped down the stairs on his bottom but did walk down the last two steps holding the therapist's hands'.

I didn't really take too much notice of it. It wasn't because I didn't respect Lindsey, because I did. It was more that the report was way out of date. Things had changed significantly.

Fraser was now walking really easily up and down the stairs. He usually needed the support of the rail but that wasn't a problem. That's why we'd put it there. The important thing was that we'd cleared that hurdle and, as was now becoming the norm, we had done it without a major drama.

It was hard to believe. A year or so ago, we would have had scenes of utter uncontrollable rage from Fraser. He would have worked himself up into a state every time I even suggested he climb the stairs. He would have been sick with anger. But the worst thing I had experienced during the past few weeks was a bit of reluctance and defiance. On the scale of one to ten with Fraser, it was a two or three at most. In other words, it was nothing.

When Lindsey returned to see Fraser a month or so later, she watched him rather proudly walking up and down the stairs using the rail.

'Gosh, he's done well hasn't he, Louise?' she smiled.

We both noticed Billy was lurking at the top of the upper flight of stairs, peeking down.

'What's he doing there I wonder? Moral support perhaps,' Lindsey laughed.

There was so much that I could have said, but I decided against it.

Instead I just smiled and shook my head quietly.

'Who knows?' I said. 'Who knows?'

Chapter 10

New Bloom

Spring in the Highlands is always a beautiful and rather magical time but in 2012 it seemed especially so. We'd been through a really long, dark and cold winter, so it really lifted the spirits to see the first daffodils and hear the gentle, rushing sound of the river, swollen with the last of the melting snow from the Cairngorms.

It felt like our fortunes were blooming a little too.

Chris and I had learned to be realistic about Fraser but the progress he'd made in the past few months had made us feel more positive than we had for a long time.

It wasn't just the calmer, happier atmosphere that had existed since we'd moved on to the Estate. We'd begun to see a lot of other encouraging signs.

Lindsey had written a really positive physiotherapy report which had found its way to the specialist orthotician who prepared his splints, a lady called Lynne in Aberdeen.

The splints had been a huge help but they were cumbersome. They stretched up the side of Fraser's leg and were also fitted under his foot, which gave him a very stiff gait. They also needed to be replaced on a regular basis, usually every six months or so, which was a nuisance.

When we travelled up to see Lynne she asked Fraser to walk around a little in his current splints then made some notes. I expected her to tell us his new splints would be ready in a few weeks, but she had other ideas.

'OK, I think it's time for you to progress from splints,' she said.

'Really?' I said.

'Yes, I'm going to get you some Piedro boots.'

'What are they?' I asked.

'They are special orthopaedic boots that support you up to the knee, but don't go under the foot like the splints. They will make it much easier for Fraser to move and bend over.'

It took a few weeks for the boots to be made but when they arrived the impact was immediate. They looked a bit like those high-ankled skating boots, without the blade obviously. But they made an immediate impact; Fraser became so much more mobile at home.

As Lynn had said, they made it easier for him to bend down and generally made him much more nimble and flexible. The first time I really noticed the difference was when he began to bounce on the trampoline, often with Billy bouncing alongside him. He also started to move much more quickly, almost to the point of running, which was an amazing progression for him.

His newfound mobility encouraged me hugely, especially as it came soon after a really interesting conversation I'd had at nursery. At first I'd been a little worried when I'd seen one of the teachers approaching me as I waited for Fraser at the end of the day.

'Louise,' she said. 'Nothing to worry about, I was just curious about something?'

'Oh, all right,' I said, still apprehensive despite the smile on her face.

'Has Fraser been studying geometric shapes at home?' she said.

I was a bit thrown.

'Erm, no,' I said. 'We've got one of those games that you have to put square, circle and triangle shapes into the correct holes, but that's about it. Why?'

'Hmm. Well today he recognised an octagon, a hexagon and a pentagon and identified them by name.'

I was shocked, but tried to make light of it.

'Oh,' I said. 'That's Fraser for you. Always full of surprises.'

'He certainly is,' she said.

I knew the school were working hard, trying to understand his special needs so that they could cater for his education in the next year as he prepared for his move to 'big school' the following August.

'Do you want me to ask him about it?' I said.

'No, there's no need to do that,' she said. 'But it would be good if you could observe him and let us know if there are any other nice surprises in store for us. It will obviously help us to mould his lessons to suit him.'

My news didn't get quite the reaction I'd expected when I spoke to Chris that evening. Rather than looking shocked or taken aback in any way, he just nodded.

'Oh he does that sort of stuff all the time,' he said.

'Really,' I said. 'When?'

'Well there was that time up with mum when we were playing that game.'

'Oh yes, the dice,' I said, suddenly recalling what had happened the previous year when we'd gone up to the coast to see Chris's mum and her partner.

They were great lovers of board games and Chris's mum had found this snakes and ladders type game in a charity shop. Like me, she had tried all sorts of toys on Fraser in the hope that one day he'd take to one of them. This one seemed to have piqued his interest. It had big pieces which helped him because he couldn't handle little objects.

As we got the game under way, Chris's mum gave the dice to Fraser. He threw it and before anyone had a chance to say anything just said: 'five'.

Sure enough, it was a five, but we were all surprised that he didn't stop to count the dots or anything like that.

It happened again when it next came to his turn.

'Six,' he said, earning himself the right to roll again.

And on it went, throughout the game.

'Four.'

'Three.'

Each time he had announced the number almost the instant the dice had landed. He just knew by looking at the number of dots.

He was three at that point and we'd never played board games or anything like that before.

'Yes, I'd forgotten about that,' I said. 'And remember when he counted backwards from twenty to one. He was only two when he did that.'

'He did a couple of things that surprised me the other day as well, I meant to tell you,' Chris said as we both now warmed to the theme.

'What else are you keeping from me?' I said, half joking.

'We were sitting in the car outside the supermarket in Aboyne while you were inside shopping with Pippa. He pointed at a house and said: "look that house has got a weather vane". I had no idea he knew what a weather vane was,' he said.

'And the other night he mentioned the word gravity. I didn't think he knew what it meant so I just said "what's gravity, Fraser?" He just looked at me and said "holds you down" and then walked off.'

We both burst out laughing. There was no way he was learning any of this stuff at his nursery. It was primarily for two to four year olds and focused mainly on play and activity. At the time they were spending most of their time collecting daffodils for a springtime project.

So the question was, where was he getting this information from? We knew that he couldn't read himself because we were still reading to him. And it wasn't television because the only programmes he watched were *Tom and Jerry*, the BBC children's channel, CBeebies, and one or two other kids' channels. He would get really upset if anything other than these programmes came on.

But that was it really. He certainly wasn't watching maths or weather or science programmes on National Geographic in secret. Well, at least, I didn't think he was. I now had my doubts.

This, again, was one of the paradoxes about

autistic children. According to the conventional measurements, they do not develop as well as other children. But often they have abilities way beyond what normal children of their age might have. It is a cliché to say that all autistic children are gifted and I didn't want him to be pigeonholed as some kind of Rain Man, reciting telephone numbers and memorising cards at the casino. But there was definitely untapped potential in him. It made me realise that he wasn't the desperate case that, I'm sure, some people imagined him to be.

It gave me a real boost. I constantly worried about what was going to happen to Fraser educationally. The words that we'd heard in Aberdeen when he was diagnosed with autism still swirled around my head every now and again. 'Fraser will never attend an ordinary school.'

In some ways we'd already defied that rather gloomy prediction. His nursery wasn't a 'special needs' school in any way. Yes, he was the only child there who needed extra attention but he was simply a member of the class most of the time. Deep down I longed to get him into a nice primary school in a class full of other children his age where he would always be treated just like everyone else.

I even pictured it in my head. I would be there, at the school gates, watching him as he headed up the steps in his uniform with a rucksack on his shoulder.

I knew it was probably far-fetched. His problems were too numerous for him to transform into a normal schoolboy, whatever that might be. But a mother could dream, couldn't she? Snippets of encouraging news like this really boosted my belief that it might just be possible. As the new spring took hold and the days began to slowly lengthen, I was more determined than ever that I was going to give him a chance.

As usual, the first flush of spring coincided with Fraser's birthday. It was hard to believe he was four. It seemed like only yesterday that he'd come into the world, screaming the walls down.

In contrast to Christmas, which he had never really 'got', Fraser really responded to his birthday. I think it was related to the fact it is focused on him. It also satisfied his need for order. He could relate to the fact that he was one year older, that he could put a number on things. In his uncertain, autistic mind I think this was important.

So I really enjoyed going through the same routine every year. It would begin the day before when I made him a special birthday cake, decorated with his name and, this year, a single candle in the shape of the number four. Then, when he had gone to bed,

I set to work decorating the kitchen and the rest of the house.

I placed the cake in the middle of the dining table with all his cards arranged around it. I then put up a big 'Happy Birthday' banner and streamers.

Chris and I then blew up balloons and put them in the lounge with all his presents. Chris also blew up a giant, helium balloon with a giant 4 on it. He then hung another couple of 'Happy Birthday' banners, one in the living room and another one on the bathroom door, the first sight that greets Fraser when he emerges from his room in the mornings.

Fraser loved the routine and was excited the moment he got up the next day. 'It's my birthday. Fraser is four,' he said, for what would be the first of many, many times.

Billy seemed to know what was happening and had arrived in the kitchen where he was fixated on the balloons. Unusually, he had also positioned himself by Fraser's chair. This only seemed to add to Fraser's excitement.

'It's my birthday. Fraser is four today, Billy,' he said between almost every mouthful of his breakfast.

We then went through to the lounge where Fraser kicked it up a gear. Chris and I had laid out a few presents. As always, it was pure guesswork. Fraser might like them, he might not, but it was still a joy to see him methodically unwrapping them one at a time.

This year we had bought him a LeapPad computer, a lovely, learning platform that allowed him to interact with games and other stuff. We'd also got him some earphones and some games.

Billy was still glued to Fraser's side, fascinated by the discarded wrapping paper which he was soon burying his nose in. When Chris playfully threw a piece of curled up ribbon across the room he darted after it as if his life depended on it. It was lovely to see him having fun along with the rest of us. He was, after all, as much a part of our family as anyone else now.

It was a normal, nursery day so I had to get Fraser ready. He didn't protest; as long as he could wear his 'I am 4' badge he was quite happy. He also knew that they would have a birthday cake for him at the nursery too, as they did for all the children. When I picked him up from nursery later, he played with his LeapPad in the lounge which pleased Chris and I no end. The previous year we'd spent a lot of money on a battery-powered police bike which he had totally ignored.

We then sang him Happy Birthday and let him blow out the candle. After that, it was a routine evening.

We weren't at the stage where we invited other children; Fraser was still detached at nursery. He was happy to sit and play with the other children but he didn't really interact. So he didn't have any 'mates', so to speak. It made me feel slightly sad in some ways but I knew that he had Pippa and his best friend of all, Billy.

We'd seen how deep their bond had become again a couple of weeks before his birthday.

Fraser had been to the doctors for his final MMR jab, to immunise him against measles, mumps and rubella. Bizarrely, he didn't have any problems with injections. You'd have expected him to be an absolute nightmare but he wasn't. He'd had more than his share of needles inserted into him over the years but never once had he kicked up a fuss. It had been the same this time.

Unfortunately, he returned home feeling really under the weather. He had been fine in the car but within half an hour of getting home he was listless and had a high temperature. I didn't call the doctors immediately; I'd been warned that a high temperature and drowsiness was possible in the hours after the vaccination. I just needed to keep him hydrated with water and make sure he wasn't sick or really over-heated. He didn't want to go to bed so I had plonked him on the sofa in the living room in front of the television.

Chris was still at work, I had dinner to sort out and Pippa was in an unusually demanding mood, so I'd only been able to keep an eye from a distance. Fortunately, Billy was on the case.

He had been outside waiting for us when we'd arrived home. Once again, he seemed to sense he was needed. I had barely put the blanket on Fraser on the sofa when he appeared. He promptly hopped on to Fraser's lap, curling up tight and lying there, pretty much motionless.

Billy was too lively a cat to lie there for long, so I assumed that by the time I next looked in on them he'd be gone. But he wasn't. About twenty minutes later, the two of them were still there, intertwined in a knot. Billy, clearly, wasn't going anywhere. It stopped me in my tracks and proved to me something that I'd long suspected.

A lot has been written about cats' ability to sense when humans aren't well. According to some they can, for instance, detect epileptic fits before they happen. Others reckon that the act of purring can actually help heal humans. It's something to do with the vibrations.

I'm no scientist so I have no idea whether there's any hard evidence to support those theories. But I do know what I saw that afternoon. Instead of roaming the grounds of Balmoral in search of voles or birds, Billy had chosen to stay indoors with Fraser. He hadn't done this for his own entertainment because there wasn't any. Fraser wasn't in the mood to roll around on the carpet or play chase on the stairs or in the garden. There had to be a reason for it?

By the time Chris got back from work that evening, Fraser's temperature had dipped a little bit. But he was still groggy and generally under the weather. So we decided to give him a light snack and put him to bed.

Billy had got into the habit of letting Fraser fall asleep and then sliding out into the night for a couple of hours. Not tonight. He positioned himself in a spot at the bottom of the bed where Fraser had curled his legs up and remained there until morning, by which time his mate was well on the way to recovery. It was only then that he felt free to stand down from duty, disappearing through the cat flap and heading off goodness knows where for the morning.

There were times when I wondered whether I was projecting too much on to their relationship, whether I was exaggerating the influence Billy was having on Fraser.

Chris was still sceptical. He didn't doubt their devotion to each other but he just saw it as a friendship between a boy and his pet, nothing more, nothing less.

At times I felt foolish, naive even. How could a cat exert so much influence over a little boy? When I looked at it in the cold light of day, it didn't really make much sense.

A couple of events that spring gave me the reassurance I needed. For the first time, I began to feel like I wasn't quite so naive – or foolish.

It was rare that Fraser was happy to hear someone knocking on the front door, but one morning he reacted to the sound by running straight into the hallway.

'Is it Kay?' he asked.

'Yes, Fraser, I think it is,' I said.

Kay was an occupational therapist who had known Fraser since he was little. She'd made an appointment to visit him again to assess his progress.

Of all the different therapies Fraser had received, occupational therapy had been the least effective for some reason. It was intended to help him deal with the day-to-day functions he needed to perform in life, from brushing his teeth to pulling up his trousers, eating his dinner to writing with a pencil. But it had become a real battleground for him and his therapists, with little progress. We had a suspicion that a lot of it was again down to his determination *not* to do things when he put his mind to it. So, for a while we'd discontinued therapy because it wasn't getting anywhere. The upshot of that was that I'd taken on the burden of teaching him a lot of those things, with mixed success. With a year or so to go until he went to full-time school, I knew we had to overcome these problems once and for all. He still had issues with using a knife and fork, holding a pencil and other things. We had to make progress on them and soon.

Because of this, Kay had only worked with Fraser when he was much younger, before he was fully diagnosed. She hadn't seen him for a couple of years and was taken aback by how much he'd come along.

To start with, Fraser engaged in a conversation with her.

'I saw you when you were a baby. You lived in your other house then,' she said.

'Was it the one where Billy came to stay?'

Kay looked at me, puzzled.

'I don't know Billy,' she said.

'He's Fraser's cat. Oh, here he is,' he said, looking at his friend who had just clattered through the cat flap in the front porch.

'Oh, hello, Billy,' she said.

I wanted Kay to see how much progress Fraser had made with his mobility.

'Show Kay how you can walk up the stairs,' I said.

'OK, come on, Billy,' he said, inviting him to climb the steps with him. In a flash Billy was up on the half landing waiting for Fraser to reach him.

They then lay there cuddling for a moment or two.

'Ah, that's very sweet,' Kay said.

There was paperwork to be completed, as usual.

So after a few more minutes observing Fraser, I invited Kay to have a cup of tea in the living room where Fraser was now lying on the floor watching television.

He and Billy were interacting as usual, rubbing their faces and cuddling each other. I thought nothing of it. To me, it was as normal a part of the day as the sun coming up.

Kay was in the middle of explaining something to me but suddenly lost her train of thought.

'Wow that's really unusual, I've never seen a child and a cat interacting like that,' she said. 'How long has this been going on?'

No one had really asked me about their relationship before. I explained how we'd taken Billy in 9 months earlier and how they'd bonded instantly.

She was amazed when I explained what had happened that first night in Aboyne. Kay had known how sensitive and scared Fraser was as a young boy and couldn't believe that he'd walked into the cage with Billy and just started playing with him without a care in the world.

I was reluctant to talk about how much influence I felt Billy had exerted since his arrival. I didn't want to make claims that would have made me look like some kind of fruitcake.

As it turned out, I didn't need to.

'Amazing creatures cats, aren't they?' Kay said. 'I've got the feeling that Billy is a bit of a hero.'

The look she gave me told me that she understood what was going on entirely.

A few days after Kay's visit I got a phone call from another old friend, Liz from Cats Protection.

She was after a favour. The charity was trying to raise awareness about the work it was doing and wanted to find some 'good news' stories about people and cats it had brought together.

'I've never forgotten Fraser and Billy and was wondering how they are getting on?' she said.

Liz, more than anyone, was someone who was going to be sympathetic so I told her all about the things I believed Billy was doing. It felt cathartic, unloading it all to someone who I knew would understand.

'Oh that's fantastic, Louise. I knew they'd be good for each other. Would you be OK if I ran a little story on it on the Deeside Cats Protection website?' she said.

'Of course,' I said.

I forgot all about it but a few days later I got another phone call, this time from someone at Cats Protection down in London. They'd seen the story that Liz had put up on our local website and wondered whether they could use it nationally.

'We are trying to raise awareness about Cats Protection but also about autism and how animals can help. It sounds like Fraser and Billy have such a special relationship and they are exactly what we are looking for,' the lady said.

I was a little unsure and asked her what she had in mind.

'Well, we were thinking of approaching the national Press to see if anyone would like to do a story on them', she said.

I asked for a couple of days so that Chris and I could mull it over. He, of course, was completely taken aback when I raised it.

'Why would they want to write about Fraser and Billy?' he said, shaking his head over dinner that night after the children had gone to bed.

'Because they think there's something powerful about their friendship and it might raise awareness about how cats can help kids like Fraser,' I said. 'If it helps one other mum who is in my shoes then I think we should do it.'

'OK,' he said. 'I can't see the harm in it, as long as it doesn't upset Fraser.'

I called the Cats Protection lady back the next day and gave her the go ahead, expecting never to hear anything again. But within about an hour she called back with some rather surprising news.

'Hi Louise, someone from the *Daily Mail* would like to talk to you,' she said.

I was shocked. I'd expected our story to be something that might make a few inches in a woman's magazine. I hadn't expected a big, national newspaper to be interested.

'Erm, OK,' I said.

A lady from the paper, also named Liz, rang me later that day and asked a load of questions. What was Fraser's condition? Why had I decided to get him a cat? How did Billy help him? What changes had I seen in him since Billy had arrived?

It was surreal. For the past few months, I'd felt like a fool for even thinking these things. Now I was blurting them to a succession of people, including a reporter from a newspaper read by millions. It was almost an out of body experience.

Liz had to check with her editor first but she said they might like to send a photographer to take some pictures of Fraser and Billy.

'I'd need lots of notice,' I said. 'I don't want anyone turning up on the doorstep unannounced.'

'Of course,' she said. 'And we'd make sure it was someone who is used to working with children like Fraser and also with animals.'

Again, I thought I'd not hear back for ages, but

within another few hours the reporter had called back and it had been arranged for a photographer, a guy called Bruce Adams, to come round to the house a few days later.

Fraser was amazingly laid back about the idea when I explained it to him.

'A man wants to come round and take lots of photographs of Billy,' I said, being careful not to put any pressure on him.

'OK,' he said, then trotted straight off to tell his mate all about it.

'A man is coming to take your picture, Billy.'

Bruce Adams turned out to be the nicest guy imaginable. He had worked with disabled children before, including a girl with Down's Syndrome who had become a clothes model. He had also worked with a lot of animals.

The Fraser of old would have been extremely wary of him, but this new model was fine. I wasn't sure if Billy was going to play ball, as it were, but he seemed to be charmed by Bruce as well. He and Fraser lay on the carpet, rolling around and rubbing each other's faces just like they did every other day of the week.

'That's fantastic,' Bruce kept saying as he snapped away for what must have been half an hour.

I had no idea whether it was fantastic or not. It was just normality for me these days.

Bruce said the paper would be in touch when the

piece was going to run. Again I told myself that it would probably come to nought. On this occasion, my caution proved well founded. March came and went and then April and May did the same. Mum and dad always read the *Daily Mail* so I got them to keep an eye out. But there was nothing. For a while I was a little upset. I'd been looking forward to seeing the photographs at the very least. But I'd soon forgotten about it. I had much bigger fish to fry.

Chapter 11

Shifting the Goalposts

The very best piece of advice that I'd received since having Fraser had come, unsurprisingly, from another mum. I'd met her around the time he was diagnosed as autistic when we seemed to be constantly travelling back and forth to Aberdeen.

She was the mother of a disabled child herself and we'd shared a coffee together a couple of times.

'Being the parent of a disabled child is different,' she told me. 'You can't plan for the future, you have to forget about your dreams and aspirations. You just have to live in the here and now.'

It seemed almost too simple to be true and it took me some time to accept it. I had, by nature, always been a planner, someone who automatically looked to the future. Maybe it was in my star sign.

But as we'd come to terms with Fraser's condition I'd understood the truth of her words. Slowly but surely, Chris and I had learned to just focus on the day to day, the here and now. It wasn't through some philosophical flash of inspiration or anything like that. We didn't read some trendy self-help book on 'living in the moment'. It was more a dawning realisation that it was actually the only realistic option we had because, where Fraser was concerned, nothing stayed the same. What applied one day might not apply the next. The goalposts were always moving.

Those wise words came back to me once again during the summer of 2012. Just when we thought we were heading in one direction, we had to move in another. The goalposts shifted, dramatically.

Fraser had always been unpredictable. His mood could change from one minute to the next, one day to the next. This was our reality. In the main, however, we'd been pretty lucky. He had remained consistent in his inconsistency, if that makes sense. We knew the things that were liable to set him off and we'd learned, through hard experience, how to deal with them. But we knew that there was always a chance he would go through periods of change. And that's precisely what happened.

It's hard to put my finger on when it began but the first sign that something was amiss came when he learned that one of his favourite helpers at nursery was leaving. She was a very bright and sunny young girl who had been blessed with endless patience, especially when it came to dealing with Fraser. She'd taken a real shine to him and he had been very fond of her too.

Cath had told me she was leaving. She'd been given a full-time job as a classroom assistant at a bigger school and, understandably, had taken it.

When I told Fraser the news it was as if she'd personally betrayed him. He suddenly announced that he didn't like her anymore. What was even worse, he began to dislike going to school because she was still there.

Going to nursery in the morning had become, in Fraser's terms at least, a pretty smooth operation. But almost overnight it became a war zone. If we arrived in the morning and saw her car in the car park he would begin to scream and thrash around. 'I don't like her,' he would shout. 'I don't want to see her today.'

It often took me ten minutes to calm him down and persuade him to go into school. On one occasion, I'd had to abandon ship and head home.

It had only been when this girl had left that Fraser calmed down a little. But the incident seemed to trigger other behaviour. It was strange, as if he had hit a brick wall. A lot of the positive things that had happened began to unravel.

The next tangible thing that happened was that he began to become more and more anxious at home. Suddenly he would arrive back from nursery saying that nobody liked him.

I'd try to reassure him. I'd tell him that so and so liked him but he'd have none of it.

'No she doesn't. She doesn't like me,' he'd say, working himself up into a real state. We hadn't seen that purple rage for a while but it began to return.

I checked with Cath to see whether he'd had any confrontations with any of the other children but there had been nothing. He didn't really interact with other children in any case, so it was hard to see how anyone could have upset him.

It seemed to undermine his self-confidence because from there he developed the idea that Pippa, Chris and I didn't like him either.

'Daddy doesn't like me,' he would say, apropos of nothing.

'That's not true, Fraser, Daddy loves you,' I'd say.

But he wouldn't have it. He'd cover his ears and scream until I stopped. This odd behaviour continued to escalate and eventually he began to feel uncomfortable and unhappy about everything. And then all his anxieties began to coalesce around one subject, his bedroom.

Chris and I had worked really hard to create a space in which Fraser felt comfortable and safe. But all of a sudden, everything we'd placed there seemed to be an issue.

The first thing he complained about was the colour of the wall. We had painted the room a very pale, almost neutral yellow. One night, as I was trying to put him to bed, he suddenly sat upright and put his hands over his ears. He then declared 'the wall is too noisy' and began screaming the place down. It was horrendous.

That seemed to tip him over the edge and he was soon complaining about all sorts of other things. A day or so later, Chris and I were woken up by the sound of him screaming. It was pitch dark and, for a moment, we thought there was an intruder, his shouting was so violent. But when we ran into his room we were told that 'flowers were falling from the ceiling'.

For a while we were flummoxed. We didn't have a clue what he meant but eventually worked out that he was talking about the glow-in-the-dark stars that we'd had on the ceiling since he was little. In the past they'd soothed him but now, for some inexplicable reason, they did the opposite. So we took them down.

Soon we were making other changes. He had a patterned quilt, which he'd been really fond of. It had Disney characters on it. One evening, as I was tucking him in, he suddenly started kicking and flailing and threw the duvet off. 'I don't like it, it is making me feel shut in,' he said.

'Do you want another duvet?' I said.

He just nodded. So I put a plain white one on.

He then objected to the water-proof 'topper' that we put on his mattress in case he wet himself in bed or had some other form of accident. Suddenly that was wrong and upsetting to him. That had to go too.

He also announced that he no longer wanted to wear pyjama bottoms because they stopped him from moving his legs and rubbing his knees together.

It became almost intolerable. Bedtime became a minefield or, more accurately, a battle zone. Bathtime had been relatively quiet in recent months but this again became a big pinch-point. He would start agitating about his room while he was still in the bath. He would complain that he didn't want to go and look at the 'noisy walls' and that he didn't want to be 'locked in' by his duvet. It was so disheartening. We'd made such great strides but now we seemed to be moving backwards.

Two things provided our salvation. The first was a book. It was called *Born on a Blue Day* by a guy who was an autistic savant. Reading it, I learned so much about autism and also saw so many parallels with Fraser.

For instance, this guy's compulsive need for order was so great that he ate exactly 45 grams of porridge for breakfast and couldn't leave the house without counting the number of items of clothing he was wearing.

Fraser's compulsion to have his Marmite on toast cut in precise triangles seemed mild in comparison.

Whenever this guy got stressed or unhappy he closed his eyes and counted. That again was something I suspected Fraser did.

The book was a revelation in lots of ways; reading it, I felt like I understood some facets of Fraser's personality for the first time. In one chapter the writer described how he could do amazing maths and saw numbers as shapes, colours and textures in his head. But he also talked about how certain colours could upset him. At one point he was given a red and yellow bike for Christmas. He would never ever ride this bike because, to him, it looked like it was on fire. He also spoke about how autistic people often confuse their different senses so that they can think they are hearing what they see, for instance. The moment I read that chapter a piece of the jigsaw fell into place; it explained why Fraser had complained that the wall colour was 'noisy'.

Since he'd made that first protest we had experimented with other colours, placing a few brushstrokes from tester tins of paint on the wall, none of which had worked. So I said to Chris one evening, 'why don't we give him the choice?'

'Worth a try I suppose,' he said.

So I got a Dulux colour chart from the nearest DIY shop and took it up to Fraser one evening.

'Which colours would you like your bedroom to be, Fraser?' I said.

He just jabbed his finger at some very light shades of blue and green. So that's what he got. Chris and I spent a long weekend redecorating. By the end of it, Fraser had a blue and green room.

Encouraged by what I'd found in the first book, I got hold of some others as well. I found all sorts of useful advice, a lot of which focused on the sense of order and tidiness that autistic people find calming.

Fraser's toys had always been out on the floor, ready for him to play with whatever took his fancy. Following the advice of one of the books, I put everything into a single toy box and then slipped that away under his bed.

I also co-ordinated the whole room in the new blue and green colour scheme. I got him a white bed set with printed green dinosaurs. I found some blue and green pictures that went around the room. Again, drawing on something I'd read in one of the advice books, Chris and I went to painstaking lengths to make sure they were at the exact same height and had the exact same gaps between them. It was a process of trial and horror at times. Fraser would suddenly object to the placement of an object and it would have to be moved. But eventually we got there and, after about six weeks, we were slowly regaining control of bedtimes.

The other thing that got us through was Billy.

More than ever, he proved our salvation. Early on he seemed to pick up on the fact that Fraser was getting agitated at bedtime. He broke with his usual time-table to hang around for much longer in the evenings.

As before, he would come into the bathroom when Fraser was agitated, placing his paws on the side of the bath. When Fraser was protesting that he didn't like different elements of his bed Billy would lay there, as if to suggest it was OK.

We often took his cue.

'Look, Fraser, Billy likes your bed,' I'd say. Or 'look Billy likes your duvet'.

Once more it helped calm Fraser down.

'Thank God for Billy,' Chris and I began to say on a regular basis.

We knew we couldn't just dismiss this setback. We couldn't brush it under the carpet. So we were referred back to a psychologist in Aberdeen who was going to assess Fraser. In advance of an appointment, they asked me to list all the things that had been going on but also to sum up the general position with Fraser.

What did I think was positive and what was negative, basically. So one evening, after Chris, Billy and I had once more struggled to get Fraser to bed, I sat in front of my computer screen and started typing. 'Update on Fraser', I wrote at the top of the page. I then started listing everything that came into my head. In a way it was a snapshot of our lives at the time. I still look at that piece of paper and shake my head in disbelief at the life we led during that period.

I began with a general overview and started with what, to my mind, was the most positive thing at the moment: nursery. He was quietly thriving there. His speech had improved a lot, even though he still spoke on his terms. He was also happy to play alongside other children although he didn't interact directly with them.

At home, his physio with Lindsey was beginning to pay dividends. He was now able to climb and descend stairs quite freely. I didn't mention that it was often Billy who encouraged him to do so.

Mentally, he was now displaying an excellent memory especially when it related to the car. If we made a journey somewhere, he would memorise the route immediately. He had also progressed, as Cath had predicted, from knowing the colours of cars to knowing the exact make and model of everything we passed on the road. 'That's a Range Rover,' he'd say. 'That's a Ford.'

There were, when it came down to it, a lot of positives. His sight was also really good, for instance. He often saw things well in advance of me or Chris. We'd doubt him, but then when we got closer it turned out he was right. He could see things that, to Chris or I, were no more than a dot on the landscape.

I also mentioned the progress Fraser was making with numbers and shapes.

There were still far too many negatives, however. It really pained me to have to spell them out but I knew I had to do it if the psychiatrist was going to be able to help us.

A lot of his problems were still sensory ones. His latest bugbear was having his hair brushed and he would have some of his most explosive meltdowns if I even tried to brush out any tangled or knotted hair.

I also outlined all the problems that we'd had with his bedroom, from the pyjamas to the colour of the wall.

He still had the ability to lose his temper and get very angry, very quickly. He could get into a real state if he didn't know what was happening so we constantly had to explain events and developments in advance.

That very day a television programme that he didn't like, *Noddy*, had appeared without warning on the screen. He had immediately covered his ears and begun crying.

I knew the doctors would also ask about the mechanical things that Fraser needed to do on a day-to-day basis, especially when he went to 'big school'. By now I was getting tired so I just boiled it down to a long list.

'Fraser cannot do: zips, buttons, laces, dressing,

undressing, use a knife and fork.' The list went on. As for potty training, one of the biggest headaches of all, I just wrote that it was 'a flat refusal'.

It was, in many ways, very dispiriting. There were so many more items in the negative column than there were in the positive. The optimism I'd felt a few weeks earlier had suddenly dissipated. I felt pretty low, but I'd soon feel even lower.

A few weeks later I put Fraser and Pippa in the car and drove up to Aberdeen for our appointment with the principal clinical psychologist at Aberdeen Children's Hospital.

It was quite unsettling from the outset. The doctor's room was clearly designed for her to assess children because there were toys scattered on the floor. Fraser, surprise, surprise, headed for a car which he immediately overturned so that he could start spinning its wheels. I'd brought Pippa with me too and she'd found a couple of dolls and started playing with them in a corner.

The doctor had a folder with what looked like the A to Z of Fraser's case notes, all the way back to the time he was assessed at the age of 18 months old as well as the more recent reports from the various therapists.

She spoke to Fraser for a while. He was in a good mood and was quite sweet with her. She then had a long chat with me, during which she asked me lots of questions about his behaviour. As usual, I was honest. It wasn't going to help Fraser if I dressed things up to be better than they were.

I told her there were three main issues – his problems understanding the world around him and how he fitted into it, the issues with self-esteem that he'd been displaying in recent weeks and, last but not least, his complete lack of interest in self-care, in particular when it came to the toilet.

We chatted about the recent problems we'd had in a fair bit of detail. She wanted to know how he got on in general with me and Chris and Pippa as well as other people. It was well documented that he had issues mixing with other children and would often isolate himself during play breaks and lunchtimes. I told her about the recent behaviour and my suspicion that it had been triggered by the departure of a teacher that he'd liked. This produced a flurry of note-taking, as if it was important. At one point I mentioned Billy and the positive influence he'd had but she didn't appear to be much interested in that.

Her main concern seemed to be steering Fraser towards 'big school' which she felt was crucial if he was to develop. We agreed that potty training now had to be the number one priority. She reeled off a long list of things that she felt I could do.

She thought I should remove nappies from Fraser during the daytime completely, 'regardless of the risks of accident'. I should then slowly remove them at night-time as well. She suggested that I place a towel on his car seat when I took him to nursery and back 'in case'. She warned me that I could expect a lot of accidents in the first two to three weeks.

With this in mind, she suggested I have 'plenty of spare pants and trousers in a special place downstairs at home and also in the car'. My mind boggled at the amount of washing and ironing this might involve but I took it on board.

There were things that I agreed with. She, sensibly, suggested that I play down any accidents and didn't 'scold or reprimand him'. She also had the interesting idea of a chart on the wall where I could insert smiley face stickers for every hour he stayed dry or didn't have an accident.

She suggested linking this to rewards. Some made sense, for instance, letting him watch a favourite TV programme. Others left me shaking my head in disbelief. 'Maybe you could link the smiley stickers to a trip to Aberdeen to see the washing machines,' she suggested at one point. The flipside of this was that I should consider removing his favourite TV programmes if he refused to co-operate.

She said I should keep all this going throughout the summer holidays and 'refuse to let Fraser undermine the system'.

I also had to make sure he was comfortable in the

bathroom by giving him privacy and the ability to relax with a favourite toy or book.

The list went on – and on. By the time I left the room my head was spinning.

Chapter 12

In Black and White

With summer under way, Chris and I decided to take a few days off to take the children down to Essex to stay with my mum and dad. It was the nearest we got to having a break.

It was another sad fact of life with Fraser that we hadn't had a proper holiday since he was born.

But it was just so difficult when Fraser was placed in an environment he didn't know. Even staying in hotels overnight to break up the journey to and from my parents' place could be a nightmare. There would be tantrums about going out, tantrums about where to eat. And because we couldn't take Billy with us, we often found it hard to defuse the situation. So Chris and I had basically capitulated. We had stayed in the caravan which Chris's mum owns on the coast at Lossiemouth on occasion. It was within easy reach of home and provided a change of scenery for a few days.

It was, again, such a contrast to life before Fraser when Chris and I regularly travelled abroad. The last time I'd been overseas was 2006. But then that's parenthood. We weren't unique in making sacrifices; every parent does.

One of the nice things about being with my mum and dad was that they were great at looking after Fraser. That meant I occasionally had a bit of 'me time', something I didn't really get when I was up in Scotland.

One day I decided to book myself a hair appointment. My dad had asked me to pop into the newsagents to get him a copy of the *Daily Mail* while I was out. I decided to do so on the way to the hairdressers, in case I had a long wait and needed something to read.

I have no idea why but, as I stood in the queue waiting to pay, I flicked the paper open. As I did so I got the biggest shock of my life. There on Page 3 was Fraser's face staring out at me.

'Oh my God,' I said, a little too loudly, drawing quizzical looks from the others in the queue.

I pulled myself together and scanned the page. The headline read: *How love of Billy the stray cat has finally brought four-year-old autistic boy out of his shell*. Beneath it was a sub-headline: *Billy has made a complete difference to the family home, bringing happiness and an air of calm*. There was a collection of photographs by Bruce Adams of the two of them together, cuddling and rubbing their faces together.

The piece by Liz was really lovely. I was quoted a lot, which made me wince, especially one line in which I said: 'It sounds crackers but it is like Billy is Fraser's guardian.'

But it was a fair reflection of what I'd been saying to myself for so long. 'Billy has made a complete difference to our family life; he's taken away the stress, he's added happiness and an air of calm, he's just been amazing,' I was quoted as saying. It was like hearing a voice that had been inside my head.

I was gobsmacked. I didn't know whether to laugh or cry, so I did a little bit of both.

I almost ran home so that I could show it to my mum and dad. They just looked at the paper, opened up on the kitchen table and read the piece open-mouthed. I showed it to Fraser too. He didn't really grasp what it meant but he was excited to see Billy's photograph.

'Billy is in the newspaper, granddad,' he kept saying for the rest of the day.

It was an amazing moment for all sorts of reasons. Every parent thinks their child is special but very few get confirmation of that in print. More than anything, however, it lifted that feeling I'd been burdened with for the past few months. I no longer had to feel guilty or deranged for believing that there was something unusual and magical about Fraser's relationship with Billy. It was now a matter of public record; it was there in black and white.

The piece put everyone in a good mood. That evening, Chris and I sat in the kitchen with my mum and dad, laughing and reminiscing.

Inevitably, we'd talked a lot about the children and, in particular, Fraser and Billy, whose faces in the *Daily Mail* were now pinned to the cork message board in my mother's kitchen.

My dad had bought a couple of extra copies of the paper and was re-reading it again. For a moment he was lost in thought.

'Yeah, he never stops talking about him does he? Billy this, Billy that. He reminds me of you and that kitten Pam next door had,' he said.

'What kitten?' I said, blank for a moment.

'That Siamese you spent every waking moment with when you were little. What was his name?'

'Frosty,' my mum chipped in, looking slightly sheepish.

'That's right, Frosty,' my dad said.

'You were just the same; you talked about nothing else for ages.'

'Oh my God, I'd completely forgotten about

Frosty,' I said, a flood of memories suddenly pouring into my head.

When I was about eleven, I'd become completely besotted by a kitten that Pam, the Siamese breeder next door, had shown me.

She was a proper breeder and was a member of the Siamese Cat Club and had a couple of 'queens' from whom she bred most years. I'd pop next door every year to see the litters, usually half a dozen or so adorable little kittens. Over the years I must have seen fifty kittens passing through Pam's home. But there was something about this one kitten that was special. It was love at first sight. He was tiny, very cute and lilac in colour and, for some reason, I called him Frosty.

I spent hours in Pam's house playing with him. I'd find an excuse and head over there straight after school. I'd then sit there making little toys out of wool yarn which I'd wrap around a piece of cardboard and turn into a ball which I'd then toss across the room for Frosty to chase around like a lunatic. I'd been a pretty happy schoolgirl, without any particular problems, but whenever I had been feeling cheesed off about something, spending a few minutes with Frosty seemed to ease all my troubles. I hadn't thought about it for a very long time but I could remember how it had been as if we'd been in a little world of our own, a bubble where my parents or my sister or my schoolteachers couldn't bother us. It had been magical.

Pam knew that we were meant to be together and offered him to me. But I knew I faced a problem in my mum who had a real aversion to cats since that cat had jumped on her belly when she'd been pregnant with me. My fears were justified. She said no, leaving me feeling devastated.

Pam had been really sympathetic and had made sure that Frosty wasn't one of the kittens she placed in other homes, which was really generous of her. These kittens were worth a fortune. But every time I went over there I could tell that the clock was ticking and he'd eventually leave too.

It went on like that for a couple of months with me trying everything I could to persuade my mum, but to no avail.

One day the inevitable happened. Pam popped round and broke the news that she'd been approached by another family to take Frosty. He was the last of the litter and was getting to the age where he had to leave or there would be behavioural problems. She'd had to say yes.

I was heartbroken. I cried my eyes out for what felt like a week. I'd been utterly besotted by this cat.

'You didn't forgive me for ages when I said you couldn't bring him into our house,' my mum said, seeing me lost in my thoughts and sensing what I must be thinking.

'No I didn't,' I smiled. 'I just thought I'd had my heart broken.'

It was strange. I'd been reminded of Pam the day Billy had arrived in his white cage, but I'd completely forgotten about Frosty until now. Maybe I'd been suppressing the memory? Whatever the explanation, even more than 25 years later, I felt really emotional thinking about him. I certainly hadn't equated my relationship with Frosty with Fraser's friendship with Billy.

'I'd honestly forgotten all about him,' I said.

'Well maybe it was a subconscious thing. Maybe that's why you knew that it would do Fraser some good to have a cat,' my mum said.

'Whatever it was, it was definitely a good move,' my dad said.

My mum and dad didn't use the internet and I didn't, at the time, have a smartphone with access to emails. So it was only when I got home and opened my computer that I saw a screed of emails about the *Daily Mail* piece. A few were from Liz, the reporter, telling me that the article was about to run. Others were from the other Liz and the lady at Cats Protection in London, both congratulating me on the piece and thanking Fraser and Billy for giving their charity such good publicity.

There were also a couple of letters, one of which was simply marked: 'Louise Booth. Balmoral. Scotland.'

The reaction was quite extraordinary. The piece was soon online and began attracting a mass of comments, almost universally positive. They reinforced that feeling of relief that I wasn't alone in believing in the power of relationships between children and their pets. 'What a beautiful cat and a beautiful boy. You are a very lucky family to have been blessed with this special animal,' one Australian wrote, summing up the general tone. 'Miracles do happen just when you need them,' another lady in America said.

Of course, there are always those who see religious connotations in a story like this and we weren't an exception. 'In certain times of our lives God sends us unusual friends to help out,' one person said.

But the comments weren't just about animals or cats, specifically. I was really pleased that, just as Cats Protection had wanted, the piece seemed to have touched a nerve about autism.

The most heart-rending comment was from a man who had struggled with the condition all his life. 'I was born in the late 40s, when very few doctors recognised autism symptoms and when being an "awkward" child only resulted in knock-out pills and stays in asylums,' he wrote. 'I was only diagnosed at the age of 60 and the support and understanding I am now receiving has finally brought me some calm, some happiness and a lot of love to give and to receive. Let's make the lives of a lot of children happier with the undemanding love of pets.' It brought tears to my eyes, not least because I knew how easy it was, even in this day and age, for an 'awkward' child to be shunted to one side. I'd suffered that myself, with Fraser.

In the days that followed we started getting fan mail and presents from far and wide. One lovely lady sent Fraser a letter and a photo of her cat, along with £20. Another sent a tea towel with a lovely image of a cat on it.

We also got offers to do other articles in the media, not just in the UK but abroad as well. But Chris and I talked it through and turned them down because we didn't want to put Fraser through too much. We weren't interested in becoming celebrities or getting rich. Most of all we didn't want Fraser and Billy turned into some novelty act.

The reaction locally was fairly downbeat, as I'd have expected. It wasn't a community to make a great fuss of people, although a few people did mention seeing the article and enjoying it.

Probably the nicest compliment we received

directly came the first day Fraser went back to nursery after our return from Essex.

'Oh hello, Louise,' Cath said when I dropped him
off.

'What a lovely piece in the paper on Fraser.
Everyone saw it. Come in and see what the girls did.'

The girls had created a sort of collage with the
newspaper article on the pin board along with photos
of Fraser. There were also some nice notes, congratulating him.

'Billy is in the newspaper,' Fraser said when he
saw it.

'And you were in there too,' one of the girls said.
'Aren't you a clever boy.'

It reminded me why I was so happy with this place.
I'd arrived back from Essex already feeling energised
and ready for the next phase of Fraser's journey. The
warmth and support the nursery always showed us
made me feel even more like my batteries had been
re-charged. It wouldn't take long for them to go flat.

Chapter 13

Alarm Bells

As I sifted through the morning post, I saw a letter with the hallmark of the nursery school. It was approaching the school summer holidays so I assumed it was an update on Fraser's progress or maybe a note about their activities during July and August, when they would remain open as usual.

It only took a second to work out it was neither of those things. I had to read it twice to believe it was true. The nursery was closing with immediate effect. I would need to make 'alternative arrangements' for Fraser's education.

I felt sick to the pit of my stomach and had to sit down in the kitchen for a minute trying to absorb what had happened.

The letter was pretty brief and to the point. It said that June 27th was going to be its last day and wished everyone well for the future. There was no mention of any alternative nurseries.

After a while I composed myself and rang Chris. He was busy rewiring a room somewhere in the main castle building so couldn't speak for long but he was as shocked as I was.

I rang around a few other parents to ask if they knew what had happened, being careful to make sure Fraser didn't overhear the conversations.

'I just don't think it was making enough money,' one mum said, sounding as devastated as me.

'There were only eight children attending regularly so the place had been running at a big loss,' another one said.

'But, to be honest, it was so good I'd have happily paid a bit more to keep it going,' she added.

I felt very much the same. I wouldn't have found the money easily but I'd have found it somehow.

Throughout that morning I kept looking at the letter, almost willing it to magically rewrite itself so that this had been a bad dream. But it didn't.

As the reality sank in I felt terribly sorry for Cath and all the staff there. A part of me felt let down by them, of course. I wished they had been able to tell me they were in trouble. After all, I'd only been in there a week or so earlier, chatting about Fraser's appearance in the *Mail*. But mostly I sympathised with them. They were such warm, dedicated people. Where were they going to get alternative jobs in a small, rural community like ours?

Inevitably though, my greatest concerns were for Fraser. It had been such a battle to get Fraser into the right nursery and Cath and her staff were doing such a great job with him, I felt like the bottom had fallen out of my world. I really felt like we'd taken one step forward and twenty two steps back. Maybe more. I felt like we were back at square one in many ways. I felt like crying. In fact, I did.

I didn't know how to tell Fraser. His worrying was, if anything, even more intense now. He would sit, rocking, while he reassured himself that everything was all right. 'It's OK, it's OK,' he would tell himself incessantly.

The thought of not going back to the nursery and, even worse, going to a new school would be like an atomic bomb going off in his life. It would throw him into a complete tailspin.

Having said that, there was a part of me that wondered whether Fraser already knew. It occurred to me that he might have already picked up on what was going on weeks back. Maybe that had been the catalyst for the long nights of hell he'd given us at the beginning of summer? Maybe it hadn't just been the departure of his teacher? Maybe he'd got wind that the nursery was in trouble? I'd probably never know. What I did know was that it presented me with a problem, a very big one.

The state schools were due to break up in a few days time and would return after six weeks in mid-August. I basically had between now and then to come up with an alternative education for Fraser.

I could, if necessary, keep him at home with me for the year. Primary school, when he was five, was compulsory. Nursery school wasn't. But I knew that was a non-starter. The only way Fraser was going to progress and develop was by interacting as much as possible with the outside world, not retreating back into the bubble that was home. It was a view backed up by all his therapists and every other expert we'd encountered. And he now needed to step up so that he was going five days a week. I needed to keep his schooling going, somehow. But where?

The most straightforward choice was the state school in Ballater but, truth be told, we didn't think it suited Fraser. This wasn't snobbishness or picki-ness on our part, quite the opposite. We knew it was a decent school which provided a good service to the local community. But we also had the feeling it would be totally wrong for Fraser, both short and long term. The nursery was part of the bigger school and would be a huge challenge for a boy who didn't like large groups of other children. It might be a retrograde step for him.

Unfortunately, I had very few options and I needed to start exploring them so the school was my first port of call. The head teacher got back fairly quickly and told me there was capacity in the nursery but, because of his needs, she would have to discuss taking Fraser in with her nursery teacher.

'I'm sure you'll understand,' she said.

I did. Completely.

In an ideal world, I didn't want Fraser to go there in any case so the delay gave me a chance to put Plan B into action.

I made an appointment to see the head of the tiny little school in Crathie. The school had been built originally in 1873 to serve families from both the Balmoral and Invercauld Estates as well as the villages of Crathie and Abergeldies. It was a lovely, traditional style school with three classrooms and a small servery where the children ate their lunch. It had a large playground with grass and hard areas as well as some woodland and an adjacent playing field. It even had its own pet rabbit. But the real beauty of the school was its class size – there were never more than 15 pupils in the entire school. Sometimes as few as a dozen children shared the two main teachers, the head and another excellent teacher, along with a classroom assistant. I'd also been to various toddler groups, prize-givings, coffee mornings and nativity plays there over the years. I liked the friendliness and atmosphere; it was very similar to the nursery in Ballater in many ways. It was a very caring and nurturing environment and I'd seen many of the Estate children go through the school with excellent results.

All in all, it seemed to me to be perfect for Fraser.

It was a short drive to the school so I popped in a few days later to have a chat with the head. I was blunt and to the point: I asked if Fraser could start full-time school instead of continuing at nursery level. My argument was simple. It was only because he missed the school cut off date by one day that he wasn't eligible to join in any case. If he'd been born a few hours earlier, on February 29th 2008 rather than March 1st, he would have been measuring up his uniform already. What difference were those few hours going to make?

The head was very sympathetic. But she said she couldn't bend the rules. The only way he could be admitted 'under age' was if he was from a military family that had been posted to Scotland and had been at school in England or Wales from the age of four. It was so frustrating. *Why had I been cursed with such a long labour*, I now thought to myself?

The good news, however, was that she was more than happy to have him continue at the toddler group. 'I'm sure we can then take him in to the big school the following August,' she said.

It was a really stressful period for Chris and me. We had been planning to manage the transition to a full-time school so that it caused Fraser – and his new school – the minimum anxiety. Now it was going to cause the maximum mayhem. We dreaded the weeks and months ahead.

Eventually we came up with a compromise plan. If they were willing to take him, he could go to the nursery in Ballater three days a week and the play group in Crathie for the other two days. If Crathie worked out we would aim for him to go there, full-time, the following August.

It all seemed straightforward. Unfortunately, we knew that, where Fraser was concerned, that wasn't a word that applied very often. He could have a problem with the other children, the teachers or he could reject the school completely. It wasn't going to be easy. But it was the same old story: the goalposts had shifted and we had to deal with it.

The nursery's final day was June 27th, the first anniversary of Billy's arrival by a strange coincidence. It was, predictably, a very emotional day.

I was absolutely devastated. In the space of 20 months or so they'd had a huge influence on Fraser.

They had been the first people to see that, behind that angry little boy, lay a really sweet, lovable personality. And they had helped him develop in lots of subtle ways. When he arrived there, he had very little imagination when it came to playing, for instance. He would simply sit and play with whatever spinning object he could lay his hands on. Now he could be creative and do things that other kids would do, like pretending he was cooking things at home. Again, it may not have sounded like much, but within Fraser's world it was a significant step in the right direction.

They had also been really important because they had given me some time to myself. The six hours or so a week they'd gifted me was precious, especially as it gave me valuable time to spend with Pippa, who as a newborn baby when Fraser had started, really needed a lot of attention.

A couple of days later Ballater School wrote back to me and said they would take him in, which was a relief in many ways. Given his nature, there was no way Fraser was going to be able to go in 'cold' to a new school on the first day of the new term. He would need a little time to get to know the environment and the teachers, if possible. So my first priority was to get him in there to familiarise himself with the place but when I tried ringing there was no answer.

The following day, however, I was driving into Ballater to do a couple of errands and decided to just drive by. I knew that the school was used occasionally during the summer. I had Fraser with me, we might be lucky, I figured. No such luck. All we were able to do was gaze at the school from the outside, which was counter-productive because Fraser started asking questions.

'Who will I sit next to? Who will be my teacher?' Afterwards I'd regretted taking him there. All it had done was heighten his anxieties. That was the last thing he – or indeed any one of us – needed.

The upheaval that was about to take place had really upped the ante and I knew there were a few things that I would need to tackle immediately.

So one morning, after Fraser had been through his normal breakfast routine and the house was quiet, I started gathering together what, to the outside eye, would have seemed a very odd collection of items. Soon, laid out on the worktop of the kitchen, was an egg timer, a picture book and a plastic potty.

Once I'd finished my morning cup of tea, I took a deep breath, placed all three items in the downstairs toilet and went into the living room to fetch Fraser. For the umpteenth time, I was going to tackle Fraser's greatest bugbear – potty training.

It was long overdue. He was now four years old and was still wearing a nappy to school, which wasn't great. When he'd started at his old nursery this hadn't been that unusual. A lot of the children there were, like him, no more than two years old and hadn't been properly potty trained. Since then, however, every other child had learned how to go to the toilet on their own. Fraser, however, had steadfastly refused to even contemplate it. Whenever Chris or I had asked him to go to the toilet without his nappy on, he had virtually screamed the house down. It was so entrenched in his autistic mind that this was how he did his toileting that he couldn't even think of doing it any other way.

Unfortunately, it had now become a real issue for us. At the old nursery, Cath had been supportive. With her experience of autistic children, she knew it would happen at some point, but that Fraser would decide on that moment. It might be next week, but it might be next year or the year after that. Unfortunately, we couldn't wait that long anymore.

There was no way I could let him go to his new nursery without being potty trained. It would be embarrassing, not just for me but for Fraser because it would make him stand out even more from the rest of the children. It would make him seem even more 'special' and not in a positive way.

As if this hadn't created enough pressure, the psychiatrist had sent me a long letter, repeating the long list of advice that she'd given me on potty training.

This time it came complete with underlined words and bullet points. It felt intimidating and, if I was honest, a little bit patronising. I had guided Fraser through a lot. I was sure I could steer him through this without being treated like an idiot who didn't know the first thing about how to raise her child.

There were things on the list that I would take heed of, but there were others I was going to ignore. I was going to do it my way.

One piece of advice that I'd been given by my sister was to introduce Fraser to a book about potty training.

'It really helped with my two boys Louise,' she said.

I was amazed at the range of books available and how imaginative they were. There were books about pirates and firemen going to the toilet and special books for children who were scared of going to the toilet. I chose a couple of entertaining ones with colourful pictures and began reading them to him at bedtime. One of them had an interesting technique involving an egg timer which was used to keep children sitting on the seat for as long as possible. That seemed to me to be the sort of thing that might work for Fraser.

The night before I told him we'd start the following morning so he wasn't completely surprised by what was happening.

I knew the key was to keep him stimulated mentally while he was sitting there so I had brought the books with me as well.

'If you sit there for five minutes, I will reward you with a biscuit,' I said.

He gave me a quizzical look as if he was checking out whether I was being honest with him. He then thought about it for a moment and just nodded.

I was so glad that no one could see me as I crouched there, sitting alongside Fraser. I felt like some kind of crazy person, holding an egg timer next to a four-year-old child who was sitting there with his nappy around his knees.

I could tell that Fraser was restless already.

'I don't want to stay,' he said. 'I don't want to.'

'Please, just for me, just until the sand runs out,' I said.

As I stared at the egg timer it was as if each grain was moving in slow motion. But then I saw the door nudge open and a familiar figure loomed into view.

Billy.

Why he'd decided to come into the room I had no idea. Had he heard us talking and been attracted to the noise? Had he picked up on Fraser's complaints? As usual, I didn't have the foggiest idea. All I knew was that I was really glad to see him and was even more pleased when he plonked himself down and placed his head gently on Fraser's shoulder.

'Look, see, Billy wants you to use the potty as well, Fraser,' I said.

To my delight Fraser sat there for the next few minutes. Before I knew it the five minutes were up.

I waited until I had repeated this operation a couple of other times before sharing my news. Apart from anything else, I didn't want to put a hex on it. I wanted this to stick.

The second time I attempted it I deliberately left the door open so that Billy could hear us. He needed no second invitation and was soon sitting there alongside Fraser once again. And once again the sand in the egg timer took an eternity to run out. But this time I gave it to Fraser to hold. He was fascinated by it and when it eventually ran out he was still sitting on the potty, stroking and talking to Billy. Even better, he'd done a wee.

'Good boy, Fraser,' I said, excitedly. 'That's another biscuit for you.'

I knew Fraser would tell Chris about this soon enough, so I couldn't resist breaking the news that

evening as we were watching TV after putting the
children to bed.

'You'll never believe it but Fraser sat on his potty
today for five minutes,' I said to Chris.

'Really?' he said, genuinely surprised.

'And it wasn't the first time he's done it. He did it
yesterday as well.'

Chris knew better than anyone how hard it had
been to get Fraser to this point. But he also knew
that we were far from home and dry, as it were.

'I think a lot of it was down to the fact that Billy sat
with him,' I said.

I could tell that he was dubious, as usual.

'Tell you what, you sit with him next time and see
how you get on,' I said.

'OK, why don't I do it before bedtime tonight?'

An hour or so later, while I was sorting Pippa out,
I heard Chris heading up with Fraser. Almost immediately, I heard the distinctive sound of the cat flap in
the porch.

When I poked my head out into the corridor, I saw
a flash of grey and white disappearing up the stairs. I
was downstairs with Pippa and took a few minutes to
sort her out for bed. By the time I went upstairs,
Chris was in Fraser's bedroom tucking him in to the
duvet. Billy was there too, as usual.

'How did you get on?' I asked.

'Fine,' he said.

'Did Billy come in?' I said. 'Yeah, funnily enough, he did. He kind of nudged the door open and plonked himself next to us.'

'Didn't you think that was odd?' I said, studiously avoiding eye contact.

'Yes, I suppose so,' he said, doing the same.

I knew Chris wasn't going to acknowledge it directly, but it was obvious what he was thinking.

It was a long haul over the coming weeks. Some days Fraser would sit holding the egg timer for ten or fifteen minutes. At other times he would refuse to sit there at all. As the psychiatrist had predicted, there were also accidents. Fraser got a little upset a couple of times but I heeded her advice and didn't make a big deal of it.

Slowly but surely he got more confident, even to the point of going into the toilet on his own. The only problem with that was he managed to lock himself in a couple of times!

The first time it happened I'd been in the kitchen and I'd heard a plaintive call of 'Mummy, Mummy' coming from the downstairs toilet.

He'd somehow managed to turn the lock on the door but, when he'd finished going to the toilet, had found he couldn't undo it. I tried to encourage him to try again but he'd begun to get anxious.

'Fraser doesn't like the bathroom,' he'd kept saying. 'Make it go away.'

Eventually I'd had to take drastic action and use a screwdriver to dismantle the lock mechanism. I'd found Fraser crouched down inside the shower cubicle.

Despite setbacks like this, however, he kept heading in the right direction. One weekend we drove up to Chris's mum without any accidents. I'd taken some nappies with me just in case of any setbacks but Fraser hadn't needed them, much to everyone's delight. As the summer holidays drew to a close and the new school term loomed into view, I felt quietly confident that we had dealt with another challenge. I could take a breath and prepare myself for the next one – his new nursery.

With a day to go until the start of term, we finally got an opportunity to check out the new nursery at Ballater School.

We'd had a good chat with the school to explain Fraser's condition and why it was important he familiarised himself with the school in advance. They'd invited us to pop in to have a look around when the teachers got back from their summer break. Unfortunately that was just 24 hours before the school bell rang for the first time that autumn. It wasn't ideal.

Fraser was a little apprehensive in the car on the way over and didn't say too much. We had brought Pippa along and the four of us parked outside and headed into the modern building, in the shadow of Craigendarroch, the mountain that looms over Ballater.

The school was built in the 1950s but still looked pretty modern and was arranged with a large hall and a long corridor with classrooms on one side. Fraser had never been great with corridors and started reassuring himself the moment we started walking down it, with good cause as it turned out.

All of a sudden a very loud bell started ringing. It was the telephone in the school office but it had been attached to a system so that it could be heard all over the premises. It really was deafening and made all four of us jump, but Fraser in particular was scared stiff. I had to grab him and reassure him. After that, I knew the rest of the visit was going to be irrelevant. I knew him well enough to know that the die had been cast.

The nursery teacher met us and showed us around her section of the school. Because it was part of a bigger school, catering for children all the way up to 11, it had a very different feel to it. I could sense it as I walked in but, as a highly sensitive child, I was certain that Fraser could feel it even more. He looked nervous and apprehensive and kept holding my hand for reassurance.

I didn't ask him too much on the way home. I didn't want to make too big a deal of it. I could tell that he was already worrying about it. I knew we'd have a real challenge on our hands in the days to come.

To be fair, the school made a real effort to make Fraser feel at home during his first week. On the first day he was introduced to everyone in his new, nursery class but apparently spent much of the time playing in a corner away from the others, much like he'd done at the old nursery. The day passed off without a major incident but he looked very pleased to see me and especially pleased to see Billy when he got home.

I was encouraged but it didn't take long for problems to develop.

On the third day of term I arrived at school to find him in a terrible state, crying and looking very anxious.

'What's wrong, Fraser?' I said.

'The toilet is naughty,' he said, clutching my hand.

I'd not mentioned the fact that he'd only recently been potty trained, mainly because I didn't want him to be labelled as even more unusual or challenging than he was. But I suddenly had visions of him having a terrible accident.

It turned out that it was something else.

The school toilets had one of those ceiling fans that come on automatically when the light is switched on. Fraser had been taken to the toilet with some other boys and the teacher had switched the lights on. Loud mechanical or electrical noises like that had always upset him, especially when they weren't expected, so he had had a bit of a meltdown.

The nursery teacher looked a little overwhelmed by it but I told her not to worry.

'It's not unusual for Fraser to get upset like that,' I said.

A couple of days later, however, she pulled me to one side again.

'Fraser got upset again today,' she said. 'A colleague tried to take him to the main assembly hall via the main corridor. He hadn't wanted to walk that way and got really upset when she insisted he go with her,' she said.

There was something about the way she said the word 'really' that told me he had probably screamed blue murder.

I explained what had happened with the school bell when we'd first visited.

'Oh that explains why he kept talking about the bell,' she said.

We spoke briefly about what we could do to reassure him but the problem, as always with Fraser, was that the genie was now out of the bottle. The seeds of his anxiety had been sown and they were soon taking root.

Over the coming days he began bringing his anxiety home with him. Fraser has the ability to repeat things over and over again, even when he is happy about something. But if he is unhappy about it he can go into overdrive. He can go on and on and on.

During those first days he would say the same thing 40, 50 or 60 times a day.

'I don't have to walk down the hallway,' he would say.

'I don't like the bell.'

'The fan in the toilet is noisy.'

After a couple of weeks, he had got himself into such a state that he could get rigid with fear. It was as if someone had told him to walk off the top of a 50 storey building. He couldn't sleep for more than a couple of hours without waking up to talk about it again.

Chris would get up to see him, spending up to half an hour easing his concerns or reading to him so that he could go back to sleep. It was draining for us both and there were nights – and mornings, in particular – when we simply thought it wasn't worth the effort.

Chris would be down in the kitchen at silly o'clock,

preparing Fraser's breakfast while I dealt with the protests that would come when he woke up.

'I don't like the bell, Mummy, I don't like the bell.'

We had decided against sending him a couple of times, just to give us a break. Nursery wasn't compulsory so it wasn't a problem. But we knew we couldn't do that too often. It was essential that Fraser continued to go to nursery. His therapists knew it, we knew it. If he stopped going he would retreat into his shell and, given his autistic nature, he would retreat in such a way that some or all of the progress we'd achieved would be undone. All the good work of the past year or two could go up in smoke. So we knew we had to get through this.

To be fair to the school, they worked with us closely and took action to tackle both of the big problems.

Firstly they started leaving the light – and therefore the fan – off when they took Fraser to the toilet. Then they organised it so that Fraser walked around the outside of the school if he needed to get from one end to the other. He was led through a fire exit, around the grounds and into the main hall that way, thereby avoiding the corridor.

They also called me in to discuss alternative approaches. At one point we even discussed whether Fraser could bring Billy in to school with him.

He'd already started talking about him in class and the teacher wondered whether having his best mate at his side might help him conquer his fear of the corridor and the bell, in particular.

It didn't take long for us to work out that it wasn't practicable. There were health and safety issues and it would also have drawn even more attention to Fraser. It was also unfair on Billy. He didn't really travel beyond the house and couldn't be expected to sit in a classroom for hours every day.

It was a non-starter really. Besides, Billy was busy enough dealing with the problem at home.

A few years earlier, we would have been on a downward spiral that would have been really difficult to break. The difference now, of course, was that we had our rather remarkable cat.

During those tense, very difficult weeks, he was a constant presence around us. Whenever Fraser started getting agitated about the corridor or the bell, he would appear. Often he'd be one step ahead of everyone else. Several times during that period, Chris or I headed upstairs only to find Billy was already in position, either curled up at the bottom of the bed or lying directly alongside Fraser so that he could feel his presence.

That cat's clairvoyant, I thought to myself one night.

We'd seen it all before, of course, but it was still a wonder to behold. We could try to reassure Fraser as much as we liked. But Billy could defuse a situation in seconds. By now even Chris's resistance was beginning to crumble.

'Have you noticed that Billy doesn't go out at night so much at the moment?' he said as we lay in bed one night.

For the umpteenth time since Fraser had started his new nursery, Billy had helped us calm Fraser down again.

'Mhm,' I said, sensing where he was headed.

'Which is funny really because it's probably the best time of the year for him to find things to hunt,' he said.

'Mhm,' I said, smiling quietly to myself.

'It's as if he knows when Fraser is going to kick off.'

'Mhm.'

'There's more to that cat than meets the eye,' he said, rolling over and switching his bedside light off.

'Mhm,' I said, doing the same. It took all the strength I could muster to suppress a little giggle.

Chapter 14

Tom and Billy

As the summer drew to a close, Fraser slowly settled into his new nursery. The corridor and the school bell still obsessed him but, mercifully, the amount of times he mentioned them dropped from dozens of times a day to just a few. He rarely woke up in the night to talk about it anymore.

Also, the plan for him to take the long walk around the school to avoid the corridor had paid off, for now at least. Goodness knows how he'd get on when the winter came and he had to trudge around the grounds in the snow and rain but, as usual, we'd cross that bridge when we got to it.

The two days a week that he spent at the playgroup at Crathie School had helped calm him as well. He felt very much at home there; the smaller class and more nurturing environment suited Fraser really well. It was a measure of how understanding they were that the head switched off their school bell completely when I told her in advance of the problem we'd had at Ballater. It made me even more certain that I wanted him to attend full-time school there the following August. It would give him his best chance of succeeding at school, I felt sure.

It was now several months since he'd taken that big, backward step and I had begun to feel that things were heading in the right direction once more.

One of the signs that he was making progress again was the way that his taste in television had changed. Repetition and routine made Fraser happy, so for a long time he only watched the same very childish programmes aimed at pre-school and very young babies. He particularly liked the BBC programme *In the Night Garden*, a popular show for one to four-year-olds about a bunch of colourful characters with names like Igglepiggle and Upsy Daisy who lived in a magical forest with giant daisies and other bright flowers everywhere. He watched them again and again and again. I became heartily sick of the sight and, especially, the sound of some of them. Fraser liked them because they weren't too wordy and consisted more of shapes and sounds and colours, which he probably understood more easily. But, finally, he had begun to watch slightly more advanced things, in particular cartoons. More than anything, he had fallen in love with *Tom and Jerry*, which I'd been delighted about. Who doesn't love *Tom and Jerry*?

One day I was in the living room, reading a magazine while he was watching an episode. Tom was, as usual, being outwitted by Jerry and Fraser was laughing away heartily.

For no apparent reason, he turned to me and said: 'Mummy, Billy is just like Tom.'

At first I thought he simply meant that he looked like Tom, which he did, well, a tiny bit. But then, as I sat there watching the cartoon with him, I began to see there were other, sometimes comical similarities. Of course, the most obvious was that Billy made us laugh so much.

His relationship with Toby had become really funny, for instance. The two of them had very little to do with each other in general. They gave each other a very wide berth, mainly because Toby had become, if anything, even more inanimate as he got older, spending the large chunk of every day snoozing around the house. But every now and again they'd wrestle on the carpet. It really was like something out of a cartoon. They would go through this strange ritual, like Sumo wrestlers stomping around getting ready to pile into each other. Toby would pace around swishing his tail while Billy fixed him with a stare. Then, all of a sudden, Toby would jump and land on Billy's stomach, pinning him down with his sheer bulk. They would then roll around in a big, grey ball of fur until Toby was puffed out, which didn't take too long.

Billy was much younger, fitter and stronger and I'm sure if he wanted to he could have thrown Toby off and given him a good beating. But it was just playful stuff really; there was no aggression and no yowling or screeching. Billy clearly enjoyed it and let Toby do it every time. The only downside was the mess it left. The carpet was always caked in a mass of grey hair afterwards but, to be honest, I didn't mind because it was so entertaining.

Billy had become a real entertainer in the garden too. There was a small tree in the corner which he loved climbing when he was playing with Fraser. One moment he'd be running around Fraser's feet, the next he'd be shooting up the branches like a squirrel. When he got to the top he did this funny thing where he would wrap his front and back legs around the trunk, in a big hug, letting himself sway with the breeze. Both Fraser and Pippa thought it was hilarious. He would hang there for minutes, looking down on them as they pointed up at him, laughing.

'Look at Billy, look at Billy,' Fraser would shout.

There were times when I could have sworn he did it deliberately to get a reaction.

Like Toby, Billy was always on the lookout for an extra meal so it was no surprise that food featured in a lot of his comic escapades.

One summer's day we were all in the garden sitting on the padded blanket that we'd had from the old house when Billy casually strolled on to the scene. He'd gone off after breakfast as usual and was heading back now, presumably ready to play with Fraser.

It was Pippa who spotted the state of him first then Fraser shouted 'look at Billy'. Chris and I looked round expecting him to have either caught something or be covered in overgrowth again. We were shocked when we saw his front had turned a vivid shade of yellow.

It was all the way down his bib and on the top of his legs. The kids thought it was hilarious. They obviously thought it looked like he'd been soaked in the yolk of an egg because Fraser started calling him Eggy Billy. Pippa adores her big brother and was at an age now where she tended to copy him all the time.

'Eggy Billy,' she repeated.

I took Billy inside to give him a wash. I couldn't for the life of me fathom what it was at first but after a while I smelled something distinctive. It was turmeric, the spice used in making curries. Maybe he'd been rummaging in a bin where there was a curry. The one thing I did know was that I couldn't get it out; it took a week for it to fade away.

Sometimes it was as if he would eat anything that was waved in his general direction. Not long after the curry incident, Fraser ran into the utility room where I was emptying the washing machine. I knew it must have been important because he resisted the temptation to spin the tumbler like he normally did.

'Mummy, come and look at Billy,' he said, tugging on my trouser legs.

'What is it, Fraser, can't you see I'm busy?' I said.

'Mummy come on.'

I walked into the kitchen to see Pippa sitting on the kitchen floor alongside Billy. She was clutching some Italian breadsticks.

'Here, Billy,' she said, giving him a stick, which he nibbled.

She then took it away and ate the other end.

'Give him more, Pippa,' Fraser said, rather naughtily.

'No, Pippa,' I said, lurching forward to stop her as she was about to re-insert the other end of the breadstick into Billy's already open mouth.

Part of me was horrified. *Thank goodness they were eating from different ends*, I thought, grabbing the sticks and inspecting them to make sure. But I couldn't help laughing. Chris nearly choked on his tea when I told him that evening.

Like Tom, Billy also had a habit of getting himself into the most terrible scrapes, some of them funny, some of them not. One of the funnier ones came one day when he was alone at home with Pippa. Fraser was at nursery while Chris was at work. It had all gone very quiet so I'd stood at the bottom of the stairs and called up.

'Are you OK, Pippa?'

'Yes, I'm fine, mummy. I changing Billy's nappy.'

'What?'

'I changing his nappy. He has a sore bottom.'

I'd barely set foot on the first step of the staircase when Billy came flying down the steps. He was covered in white gooey stuff which I quickly surmised was nappy cream. It was smeared all over his head and all over his back and tail.

'Billy, look at the state of you,' I said, grabbing some kitchen towel. But before I could get to him he was gone, escaping through the cat flap.

He stayed out for a few hours so that when he came back he was in a heck of mess. The cream had turned solid and rigid. He looked like a marshmallow. It took me an eternity to get it off.

Billy was, of course, capable of getting himself into more serious types of trouble and continued to do so. The scariest escapade recently had come one weekend late in the summer when we weren't around, thankfully. I dread to think how we'd all have reacted if we'd seen it.

The first hint we'd got about what had happened came when we got back from a shopping trip in Aberdeen one weekend afternoon. We were pulling up in the car when I noticed a rather nasty mess on the lawn. It caught my eye because Chris had mowed it early that morning and the grass had been looking immaculate when we'd headed off.

I had a bad feeling about it immediately.

'Uh oh. What's been going on here?' I said to Chris.

When I took a closer look I saw a big pile of animal droppings in the middle of the grass. There was a big pile of fur next to it. Moving closer, there was no mistaking what kind of fur it was. It had come from the coat of a cat.

Oh, no, I said to myself.

It didn't take Sherlock Holmes to work out what had happened. A short drive up the road from our house stood the Royal Lochnagar distillery. In the past few weeks a Labrador had appeared there. Because we lived in an agricultural area with a lot of livestock around, most people knew how important it was to keep their dogs under control. But for some reason this one had been allowed to run loose. It had been running amok and causing all sorts of trouble.

On more than one occasion, it had jumped over our low, garden fence and started going to the toilet on our lawn. I'd seen it through the kitchen window one morning and run out to shoo it off. It had hurdled the fence and run back up the hill towards the distillery.

'That flippin' dog has come into the garden again,' I said to Chris. 'Looks like it has attacked one of the cats, probably poor old Toby.'

It was logical to assume it was Toby. We had been enjoying a spell of warm weather and Toby had begun venturing into the garden where he'd lay in a corner soaking up the sun. He was older and slower than Billy so wouldn't have been able to avoid the Labrador if it had appeared suddenly. Billy was too wily and feisty to have been caught out, I felt sure.

Neither of the cats were in the utility room at the back or in the porch so, as soon as I'd got the shopping and the children indoors, I headed upstairs to make sure they were OK. To my surprise I found Toby snoozing in his usual spot, near a radiator in our bedroom.

I knelt down to check him. He seemed absolutely fine.

'Looks like it was Billy who was in the fight,' I said to Chris who was already clearing the mess from the lawn before the children came out to play.

'I'll take a look around once I've finished this,' Chris said.

'Why don't I make our tea and once we've eaten I'll give you a hand,' I said. 'You never know, he might have turned up by then in any case.'

An hour or so later, however, there was still no sign of Billy. It was a lovely, sunny evening and the birds were singing in the trees. Chris and I decided to split up; I headed up the road towards the distillery while he hopped on his bicycle and headed on to the Estate.

It was another needle in a haystack job. Billy could have been absolutely anywhere. But I was really worried about him so I was determined to at least try to track him down.

I knew I couldn't leave the kids for too long, however, so I kept popping back inside to check on them. After about three quarters of an hour heading back and forth I'd had no joy. Chris was back soon afterwards, again with no news of Billy.

'Maybe he's hiding and waiting until dark,' Chris said unconvincingly.

Neither of us was able to relax. Fortunately, Fraser was now used to Billy's disappearances, especially at night, and had gone to sleep.

We were just heading upstairs for the night when we heard the distinctive clanking sound of the cat flap.

I opened the front door and saw Billy limping in, looking very much the worse for wear. He had clearly been in the most fearsome fight. All his fur was missing from a chunk of his body. The dog must have grabbed him around the middle. Fortunately he was grazed but not punctured so I got a bowl and cleaned up all the grazes.

All sorts of thoughts went through my head as I dabbed gently away at his wounds.

Goodness knows what sort of scene had unfolded while we'd been out that day. It might well have resembled a much bloodier and realistic version of Tom fighting with Spike the dog in the *Tom and Jerry* cartoons. I was so glad Fraser hadn't seen it; it would have traumatised him. More than anything, I was grateful Billy had emerged in one piece.

The next morning he seemed fine. After breakfast, he limped into the living room and lay with Fraser as if nothing had happened. Fraser noticed the marks on his back but didn't say anything. He was just extra gentle with him. Billy must have been feeling pretty sore and probably would have rather been sleeping in the utility room than playing. But he was there for his friend. That was the other way in which Billy was like Tom, of course.

Tom and Jerry's storylines weren't always about Tom's futile attempts to capture Jerry. There were also a lot of episodes where the pair showed genuine friendship and concern for each other's well-being. Billy showed the same sort of devotion to Fraser, sometimes above and beyond the call of duty.

As the dog fight had illustrated once more, Billy was a wild character who knew how to look after himself. Yet he let Fraser treat him as if he was a toy sometimes. Hilariously, in recent weeks he had even begun to let him carry him around like a rag doll.

The first time I'd seen it I'd nearly choked on my morning coffee.

'Fraser, what are you doing? You are going to hurt Billy,' I said, seeing him holding Billy up by the belly.

'No, I'm not, he likes me picking him up,' he said. 'Look.'

He then proceeded to put Billy down and show me. He bent down, put his hands under Billy's belly then stood up so that Billy was hanging there, limp.

'And he likes me carrying him. Look,' he said, before shuffling along, swinging a floppy and completely unfazed Billy as he went.

I was amazed for all sorts of reasons. First, we had been trying to get Fraser to carry things using both hands for years but he found it very difficult because of his hypotonia. He could barely carry a cup and a plate into the living room from the kitchen. Several times he'd dropped them whilst trying. We'd also given him a rucksack to carry to nursery but he would almost fall over from the weight of it.

So to see him carrying Billy around like that was stunning. He did it once when my mum was visiting and she was left speechless.

What was almost even more remarkable was the fact that Billy let him do this. If Pippa or Chris or I had tried to do it he would have struggled away from us, I know it.

It was a measure of how deep their bond now was, how much they trusted each other. They'd turned into their own version of Tom and Jerry, Fraser and Billy.

Chapter 15

The Monster Mash

Night had fallen over Balmoral but the Estate was bristling with life. Families in bobble hats and luminous jackets were walking the grounds towards the castle, shining torches to illuminate their way. Every now and again the silence was punctured by the bang of a firecracker or the whizzing and crackling of a rocket taking off and exploding somewhere in the distance.

It was Halloween and it felt like everyone on the Estate was getting ready to celebrate – even us.

The tradition apparently dated all the way back to Queen Victoria who had taken part in a grand, torch-lit procession every October. Along with hundreds of the Estate's gillies, gamekeepers, servants, tenants and their families, she would walk to the castle where a giant bonfire would be lit each Halloween. I'd read reports about it in a history of the Estate and it sounded like quite a party. The revellers drank toasts to the monarch, danced reels and even burnt effigies of witches and warlocks. Apparently, Victoria loved seeing everyone dressed up in macabre costumes and it was regarded as one of the highlights of the Balmoral calendar.

The ritual had survived for more than a century even though the Royal Family no longer joined in. The younger members of the family often popped up to the Estate to celebrate Halloween but they tended to have parties in the private hunting lodges that dotted the vast Balmoral landscape. The castle party was now largely for the Estate's staff and their families.

In the past, Fraser had mixed feelings about Halloween. During our first year in Scotland, when we'd just moved in to the gate house, I'd wrapped him up in a warm coat and taken him to see the story-teller dressed as a witch who entertained children in a hut near the castle. He had loved it. He'd also enjoyed the small firework display they put on. Unfortunately, he hadn't felt the same way about the annual party the staff organised for the Estate's children each Halloween so we had always given it a miss. The Fraser of old didn't do large parties with children he didn't know, especially children dressed as young Dracula or Frankenstein.

So his attitude this year was a real measure of the strides he was making. Maybe it was something to do with his play group where they had been making a particular fuss, carving out pumpkins and making pointy, witches' hats but for some reason, mid-way through October, he'd started asking questions about it.

'What happens on Halloween?' he'd asked me one morning.

Fraser didn't like *Scooby Doo* or other scary cartoons and would be terrified at the prospect of 'trick or treating'. Strangers coming to our door had always been a problem and there was no way on earth Fraser would be able to knock on someone else's door, even if he knew who was likely to open it. So I highlighted the aspects of Halloween that I knew would appeal to him instead.

'Oh, it's just a special night when people get dressed up, go to see a bonfire and fireworks and the children get lots of sweets,' I said. 'You've been before, remember the witch who read you a story?'

'Yes. Can Fraser dress up this year?' he'd replied.

'If you like.'

'Can Fraser have a costume?'

Of course, Fraser being Fraser, he'd changed his mind several dozen times since that first conversation, not just about his costume but about whether he still wanted to go. Half an hour before we were due to leave he had persuaded himself he was staying home. He'd heard a commotion outside as one of our neighbours got ready to head up to the castle and had worked himself up into a state, covering his ears. Fortunately, we had back up in the form of Billy who was hanging around as usual at that time of the night. Fraser curled up on the living room floor with him for a few moments and the panic soon subsided.

So now, with an hour or so to go until the festivities began, he was happy.

I had even managed to dress him in fancy dress. He was wearing a red, skull-and-crossbones bandana and eye-patch, a waistcoat with the same design and a white t-shirt with a skull on it. He didn't look the remotest bit scary, in fact, he looked adorable. I couldn't resist taking a photograph of him.

Chris had arrived home from work and was getting changed. We were both really looking forward to going out. There weren't many nights of the year when everyone on the Estate got together without too much formality and some of our friends had already rung asking if we were still going. They knew how volatile the situation could be with Fraser.

'Looks like we are coming – at the moment,' I'd told one of my friends.

The children's party was due to start shortly before

7 p.m. so, at quarter to the hour, we grabbed a load of torches and glow sticks, then wrapped a couple more glow sticks on Pippa's buggy and headed off into the night.

We met other families on the road through the Estate, each with their excited kids. Fraser chatted away most of the way to the castle, his excitement levels climbing each step of the way.

The festivities began with torch-lit games in front of the castle. Each of the children was given glow sticks, which Fraser loved, and then asked to play a crazy game called 'Runaround'. Fraser joined in, doing his best to keep up with the older and quicker kids. He was rewarded with a handful of sweets which he tried unsuccessfully to stuff into his already bulging pockets.

'Fraser likes sweets,' he said, repeatedly for the next few minutes.

Afterwards we headed to an old pavilion near the gardens where the story-telling witch was sitting in wait. Pippa and Fraser sat on the floor of the tent with a group of other children, listening intently to her tale. She then handed out some more sweets, drawing squeals of happiness from Pippa.

From there we headed over to the Estate's cricket pitch where the staff had arranged a fireworks display. It wasn't exactly the closing ceremony of the Olympics, it was just a few dozen rockets, but it was fun and, more importantly, Fraser loved it. As the first rockets signalled the start of the display, Pippa was in her buggy and Fraser was sandwiched between Chris and me, holding each of our hands.

Again, I couldn't but help thinking back a year or two. Fraser wouldn't have been able to walk the grounds and he would have been far too nervous and sensitive to watch the explosions. As he joined in the *oohs* and *aahs* that greeted each glittery explosion, Chris and I exchanged one of those looks that needed no explanation. These were the sorts of moments we'd dreamed of sharing when we first had children. We'd had precious few of them but it had been worth the wait.

The night was still relatively young and both children were clearly having a ball. So we headed into the building which houses the gift shop during the tourist season and joined all the other families for the children's disco and party.

The staff had organised sandwiches and crisps and fun, Halloween-style drinks like Bat's Blood, which Fraser guzzled down. Pippa was sitting in her buggy but was fascinated by what was going on. I gave her a snack and a drink and left her with the other children.

There was some mulled wine and nibbles there too for us adults so Chris and I took the opportunity to catch up with a couple who we knew from the Estate.

We were chatting away happily over a cup of mulled wine when I caught a glimpse of Fraser.

'Chris, look,' I said, tugging at his shirt.

One of the housekeeping staff from the castle had started playing some suitably spooky music for the children to dance to. Fraser was in the middle of the small dance floor, dancing away to that old hit, 'Monster Mash' by Bobby 'Boris' Pickett and the Crypt-Kickers.

Where he'd learned to dance, I had absolutely no idea. But he was doing a great job, balancing beautifully on his Piedro boots, doing a cross between a jig and a reggae dance. He could have been a member of a ska band or a mini version of Suggs from Madness, pumping his arms and arching his back rhythmically to the music. He was having the time of his life.

Neither of us had a Smartphone so the moment wasn't recorded for posterity, well, on camera in any case. No matter. It wasn't an image I was likely to forget in a hurry. It will stay lodged in my memory for years to come. It was wonderful.

The fun and games were all done by 8.30 p.m. or so. As we walked back in the dark, our glow sticks and torches tiny pinpricks in the vast, darkness of the Highlands, we were all in high spirits. It had been, without doubt, the best family night out we'd ever had together here at Balmoral.

Fraser was still talking about the disco and the Bat's Blood.

'Fraser did the Mash,' he said.

'You did, Fraser,' I said. 'You are a really good dancer.'

It was way after Fraser's normal bedtime and I could tell he was tired but it didn't stop him chatting away to Billy for so long that Chris and I eventually had to separate them.

'Come on you, you've got play group in the morning,' I told Fraser, while Chris grabbed Billy and dispatched him down to the utility room.

'Halloween is nice, Mummy,' Fraser said as I tucked him into bed.

'It is, Fraser,' I said. 'It is.'

Chris and I sat up for a while, chatting about the events of that evening. We were over the moon. Fraser had behaved in a way that we wouldn't have imagined possible a year or two earlier. He had dealt with crowds, loud bangs and explosions but, even more impressively, he had joined in a social occasion which was, to us, amazing. He'd even done some dancing.

'Where did that come from?' Chris said, laughing when I reminded him of Fraser's Monster Mash.

Not so long ago, the idea of him dancing so confidently and unselfconsciously would have been unthinkable. He would have been more likely to roll around on the floor screaming like a banshee. Somehow, we were breaking down the barriers. He was coming out of himself more and more and becoming a normal, fun-loving boy in the process.

'We've just got to keep on doing what we're doing,' I said.

Chris just nodded and smiled.

'It's hard, but we are getting somewhere, I know we are.'

That night, I lay in bed, my mind turning things over and over. This time, however, it was with a happy heart. I felt very positive.

As his first term at the new nursery and Crathie drew to a close, Fraser was making really good progress. There was no doubt that being exposed to other kids five days a week was having an impact. The teachers at Crathie in particular were really encouraging him to come out of his shell. And, then, of course, there was Billy. He was part of this equation, I had no doubt. What part? Well, that was anyone's guess.

There were times when I'd sit in the kitchen, simply looking at Billy trying to work out his secret. He wasn't one of these famous cats that did 'high fives' or played the piano on the internet. He wasn't particularly cute looking; in fact, he was distinctly rough around the edges. But he had qualities that, to us, at least, were out of the ordinary. The more we got to know him, the more extraordinary he became.

It was his understanding of Fraser that really left us shaking our heads at times. There was no doubt in my mind that Billy sensed things way beyond our comprehension, in particular, when it came to our health. We'd seen it when Fraser had reacted badly to his MMR jab a while back and we saw it again, a few weeks after Halloween, when the weather turned really cold.

I was downstairs in the kitchen making a nice dinner for me and Chris but had put the baby monitors on to listen to the children. Fraser seemed to have picked up a bit of a cold so I'd given him some Calpol and taken his temperature. It seemed fine but I'd booked an appointment with the doctor the following day, just to be on the safe side, given his asthma.

I'd left him tucked up in bed, nodding off. He was clearly tired and in need of a restful night's sleep. I was busy clearing up when I noticed that I couldn't hear Fraser snoring or breathing in the monitor. Instead, all I could pick up was the persistent sound of a cat going 'meeeow, meeeow'.

'What's he up to now?' I said, slightly annoyed at Billy for disturbing Fraser.

I arrived in Fraser's bedroom to discover Billy walking around the bed in a rather agitated state. It was as if he was patrolling it, like some neurotic night watchman.

I saw Fraser was fast asleep so I didn't want to wake him.

'Come on, Billy, that's enough,' I whispered and put him in his normal position, curled up at the base of Fraser's bed.

I then headed back downstairs to carry on cooking.

I'd barely been there two minutes when he'd started meowing again.

By now Chris had appeared from outside, where he'd been fiddling with the car. He was covered in grease and oil.

He immediately picked up on the noise.

'Who's that? Billy?'

'Yes, he's agitated about something, I've no idea what.'

'I can't go up like this,' he said, showing me his blackened hands. 'You're going to have to shift him otherwise he's going to wake Fraser up.'

Rather grumpily, I headed back upstairs and scooped up Billy. I then brought him downstairs and put him in the back porch area because I knew if I left him anywhere else he'd go straight back up to Fraser's room. Even then he spent the next hour or so pacing around rather manically. I left him to it. I headed to bed early that night, none the wiser as to what it had all been about.

The next morning I took Fraser to the doctor, as arranged. I'd imagined he had nothing more than a winter cold so I nearly fell off my chair when he ran some tests and examined his throat then told me he had tonsillitis.

'Yes, he's going to have to take a course of antibiotics and remain inside in the warm for a week or so, at least,' the doctor said.

'Good job you spotted it was something serious Mrs Booth,' he added.

I didn't dare tell him that the expert diagnosis had actually been performed by our cat.

Chapter 16

Christmas Cheer

A thin, Wintry sun was still struggling to break through and there was a heavy mist hanging over the banks of the river Dee.

Chris and I strapped Pippa and Fraser into their seats, crammed the last of the suitcases and presents into the boot of the car then headed off into the dawn. We had a long journey ahead of us.

We were making the 400 mile trip down to Essex to spend Christmas at my mum and dad's house.

I had always been a family person and loved spending Christmases with my mum, dad, sister and her family. But, as usual, the excitement I was feeling was tempered a little by the knowledge that for the next eleven hours or so, Chris and I would be faced with not just the Scottish weather and unpredictable roads but the even less predictable Fraser.

Travelling remained one of the few areas where Fraser had made little to no progress over the years. Even Billy couldn't exert any influence.

It was ironic really because Fraser actually adored cars and spent much of his time spotting them and reporting on the different makes. But he also had a whole raft of idiosyncrasies which could still result in temper tantrums and screaming.

He was not, for instance, happy to have direct sunlight on his face and could get very upset if we had to drive directly into the sun during the summer. On more than one occasion, Chris had been forced to pull in to the side of the road to wait for the sun to disappear when we'd been driving back along the Dee valley at the height of summer.

Sunglasses weren't an option because he didn't like the way they felt on his head and refused point blank to wear them. So we'd had to buy a rather expensive set of special, mesh blinds that blocked out the sunlight on his window. That was, to be honest, one of his more minor complaints.

At one point, when Chris had needed a car to travel to work, we'd had two cars: a black Mazda and a grey Renault. Fraser much preferred the black Mazda and insisted on travelling in it.

In the past year or so, he'd become increasingly

anti the grey car which was interesting because, unknown to him, it had been involved in an accident involving Pippa and me but not, thank goodness, Fraser.

I'd been driving back from Ballater during the winter and hit a patch of black ice on a really twisty stretch of road flanked by trees. I'd completely lost control and the car had spun through 360 degrees and ended up on a bank, by the grace of God, between two large trees. If I'd been a couple of feet to either side I'd have gone straight into one of them and could easily have killed myself and Pippa. We emerged unscathed but the car didn't fare so well. As it careered off the road, it had ridden over the top of a couple of tree stumps and had basically been wrecked underneath.

The car had been sent away for six weeks to be repaired, which was when Fraser really went off it. It was as if he picked up on what had happened, even though we didn't tell him.

When we moved to our house on the Balmoral Estate, we'd only needed the one car so I'd sold the Mazda, much to Fraser's annoyance. There had been times when he'd said 'I don't like this grey car' continuously from Balmoral to Ballater. But, as with other problems, it had calmed down – eventually.

In an ideal world, of course, we wouldn't have had

to make the long drive down to Essex. Aberdeen Airport is an hour away and has regular services but flying wasn't an option unfortunately. Not after what had happened when Fraser was coming up to his second birthday.

If I had to compile a top five of the worst moments of my early days with Fraser then my flight back home from Luton to Aberdeen would definitely be among them. At the time it would definitely have been number one.

Fraser was just approaching his second birthday at the time and we had flown down early on a Saturday morning. All had been fine and mum and dad had met us at the airport.

It had been when they drove us back to the airport a week later that the problems began.

Mum came into the terminal with me to help me check in. She had held Fraser while I handed over our tickets and suitcase and everything was fine at that point.

But when we had to go up an escalator to head to the departures lounge, the mood changed. In fact, all hell broke loose. Looking back on it, I think it was the sounds of the wheels on the suitcase that I took as hand luggage. It was making a rumbling, squeaky sound; just the sort of sound that could irritate him.

Fraser was in a buggy and quickly worked himself into such a frenzy that his forehead was burning hot.

As we went through the security check area, I sensed people shuffling away from us. I also sensed a lot of them looking at me with disdain.

'Why can't she control him?' their faces were saying.

We then ended up in this massive, snake of a queue. When we got to the conveyor belts that fed into the security scanners they wanted me to take him out of the buggy.

I was on my own so I asked someone for help but no one volunteered. Somehow I managed to collapse the buggy and put it on the conveyor along with our hand luggage.

But then Fraser kicked up another gear entirely. It was so bad that one of the security guys there asked me whether I needed to see a doctor!

Thankfully someone took pity on me and put the buggy back in position for me to place Fraser in it again.

But then we had to queue again on the stairs leading to the tarmac where the plane was waiting for us to board.

It was hideous. When you are in a situation like that, no one wants to engage with you, no one even wants to look at you to be honest. You feel like a total leper.

By the time we were sat on the plane, Fraser was a soaking wet mess. He had worked himself into such a state he had sweated so much his clothes were literally dripping.

A friendly air stewardess had given me a wet cloth with which to cool him down. But it couldn't wipe away the memory and when I'd met Chris at Aberdeen airport I'd sworn that I'd never go through it again.

And so it was that we were on the road at the crack of dawn a few days before Christmas this year. We had learned to make the journey as pain free as possible and had got into a routine that seemed to work for us.

We did the trip in one long drive and made three long stops on the way down, usually at Stirling, still in Scotland, then somewhere around Carlisle and then finally around Lancaster on the M6.

To avoid trouble we avoided taking Fraser into the toilets at the service stations because they had those noisy hand driers which really upset him. In years gone by, I'd simply changed his nappy at each stop. But now he was toilet trained, I had brought a potty with us that we used in the car. We chose stops where there were special family toilets so that I could dispose of it.

This year, the journey passed off reasonably well. This was partly because, for the first time ever, Fraser was a little bit more engaged with Christmas this year. Along with the rest of the toddler group at

Crathie, he'd taken part in the Nativity at the adjoining Crathie Kirk, the Royal Family's church. He'd played a sheep and even sung along in the chorus – no mean achievement for him.

The school had been great in the run up, taking him and the other children into the imposing church before the actual service so that they weren't intimidated. I must admit I felt a little tear welling up when I saw him on stage along with the rest of the little ones. I'd written off the idea of him in a Nativity Play. It was another one of those dreams that I was now beginning to quietly rekindle.

He'd also enjoyed himself much more at the official Balmoral children's party this year. He'd been particularly pleased with his present from the Queen that year, a toy called 'Go Mini Crew', a Mini-Cooper car on a ramp with a steering wheel and a button that made the car jump off when you pressed it.

Adding to his excitement as we travelled down, he was really looking forward to seeing my sister's boys who were coming over for Christmas itself.

Chris and I shared the driving and we made good progress. We arrived at my parents' house early evening in time for dinner.

Fraser had always been very comfortable at my parents' place. He felt safe and very secure there. She had a meal ready for us and he ate happily, chatting away openly while feeding himself with a spoon, something he'd learned with the help of Lindsey in recent months.

The conversation revolved entirely around two subjects – the cars he'd seen on the motorway on the journey down from Scotland, and Billy.

It was an almost endless procession of one liners.

'Fraser loves Billy, granddad.' 'Billy's my grey cat.' 'Billy caught a mouse.' 'Billy goes up the tree.' 'Billy's naughty.'

Fraser always slept well at my mum and dad's house partly, I think, because his brain got so tired travelling there but also because it is so much busier and intense there than it is in our little home in the Highlands. It was one of the reasons why I was glad we lived there. Fraser wouldn't be able to cope with the speed and bustle of life in the southeast of England.

So, no sooner had he been given some supper by my mum than he was heading to bed, along with Pippa with whom he always shared a room at my mum's house. He went to the toilet and brushed his teeth before saying goodnight. I let Chris read him a story as he always did while I caught up with my mum and dad over a cup of tea in the kitchen.

No one was better placed to judge how Fraser was progressing than my mum and dad. Like Chris's mum they saw him regularly, every couple of months or so, which meant they could always tell quite quickly how he was developing. They had seen the ups and downs, the triumphs and the setbacks at first hand. My mum and dad, in particular, were plain-speaking people. They wouldn't sugar coat the truth and had been pretty blunt with me in the past, particularly when I'd been struggling but refused to admit I needed help.

Tonight, however, they had nothing but positive words.

'We can't believe how much he's come along since we last saw him,' my mum said.

'Well he'd really been in the wars then,' I said. 'It was during the summer when everything went to pieces.'

'Yes, I know but even allowing for that, he's like a different boy. He's so much happier.'

They had long ago learned to make special arrangements for Fraser and had been prepared for the usual complexities. But they had been amazed at the fact that he was walking and talking and engaging so well. The fact that he was now going to the toilet on his own and eating without a bib, using his own knife and fork, was a revelation.

'Do you know the best thing you ever did, Louise?' my mum said. 'Getting him that cat. Getting him little Billy. I think that's made such a difference to his life.'

Chris soon reappeared and the conversation moved on. But their words stuck with me throughout the Christmas holidays.

If I was honest, I still felt slightly silly placing so much importance on Fraser's relationship with Billy. Even after all the publicity earlier in the year, there were times when I wondered whether he really had helped me in as many ways as I imagined. Was I simply an over-analytical and slightly neurotic mum, looking for explanations where they didn't exist? Of course, I'd never know. What I did know, however, was that – by coincidence or not – the progress Fraser had made since Billy's arrival was real and not imagined. Those who knew and loved Fraser could see it. And that was all that mattered. It felt like I'd already been given my first Christmas present so I decided to give mum and dad theirs.

I gave Chris a look and he nodded.

'Actually, we've got a bit of news,' Chris said, a little nervously.

Mum and dad looked at me, then each other, then back at Chris.

'What?' my dad said.

Chris nodded at me to carry on.

'I'm expecting,' I said.

We hadn't been sure whether to share the news but everyone was in such good spirits that Chris and I had decided to come out with it. I knew it was probably a bit premature but I was now around 8 weeks pregnant. I'd had one little scare in the run up to Christmas. I'd passed out in the kitchen and been rushed up to hospital in Aberdeen in an ambulance but it turned out that my blood pressure was really low. I felt fine now.

My parents knew that Chris and I were keen to have another child, even though I'd been through so much giving birth to both Fraser and Pippa. We'd been ecstatic when the doctor had broken the news to me, at the beginning of December.

My news meant that Christmas was even more of a celebration than usual. Everyone was in a particularly festive mood. My sister arrived on Christmas morning with her husband and two sons who were, at seven and 10, just over two and five years older than Fraser. They got on great and the boys seemed to transmit some of the excitement of Christmas to Fraser.

He got given a range of presents which, as usual, he paid little real attention to. He was more interested in talking about Billy and telling his cousins how Sandy and Cilla and their grandson Murray were around the house feeding him.

'Murray likes Billy,' he said a few times.

There were certain parts of Christmas that Fraser could take or leave: Christmas crackers, for instance, mainly because he didn't have the strength to pull them. But he always enjoyed hearing the terrible jokes inside and always wore a paper hat.

The thing he loved most, however, was Christmas

food. This year he ate everything, including the turkey and all the trimmings and a chocolate button mousse for pudding.

That night we watched a little television then played charades for a while. Fraser joined in, even though he spent a lot of the time running around the room laughing and didn't really have a clue what it all meant. Well, apart from once.

At one point I decided to do something slightly off the wall, for a laugh. Well, it was Christmas.

'I'm fed up with doing films and books,' I said. 'So this time I'm going to mime an animal.'

Mum, Dad, Chris and my sister looked at me a little strangely at first. They began shaking their heads even more when I emerged from the kitchen with a breadstick.

'OK, here we go,' I said.

I started the usual way, placing one finger on my arm to signal that it was 'one word', but then improvised by sticking two sets of two fingers behind my head, rabbit style.

'Animal,' my dad said, still not convinced where I was going with this.

I then started sharing the breadstick with Pippa.

'There you go, Pippa, take a bite. Good. Now a bite for me. Good.'

'Who's that?' I said, drawing looks of bewilderment from everyone, apart from Fraser, who had suddenly stopped running around the room and had his mouth and eyes open as wide saucers.

'It's Billy,' he said, drawing cheers from everyone.

He talked about it almost the entire way back to Scotland.

Chapter 17

The Sixteenth Sense

The New Year was only three weeks old and a sudden blast of Arctic weather had transformed Balmoral into a winter wonderland. The grounds were a blanket of white and the castle resembled something out of a Disney movie. Its granite turrets looked like they had been dusted with icing-sugar.

Our garden was layered in a thick, flaky snow as well, so Chris, Fraser, Pippa and I had headed out to do what families do in this kind of weather – build a snowman.

Chris was doing all the rolling and building while I watched on with the children. Fraser had never been particularly interested in snow but he was out too, walking around in his latest set of new 'Piedro' boots.

The only members of the family who weren't joining in the fun were Toby and Billy. Toby's absence indoors was predictable; it was far too cold and uncomfortable for him. Billy, on the other hand, had come outside but he was behaving in a really erratic way. Every now and again he would race across the garden, stop dead about six feet away from me then pounce at my feet and then hare off again. It was really weird. He wouldn't do it to Pippa or Fraser or Chris, only to me.

Chris and the children actually thought it was really funny.

'Billy's going mad, Billy's going mad,' Chris shouted, throwing a snowball in his direction.

We just thought he was a daft cat who was excited at seeing some snow although, growing up in the Highlands, it couldn't have been his first exposure to it. We reckoned he had been born in 2010, which had been a year of particularly hideous snow up here. I didn't give it any more thought.

With the Hogmanay celebrations out of the way life had become pretty slow, which was probably no bad thing for me. I was just coming up to 12 weeks in my pregnancy and I was feeling really, really tired. My blood pressure had been fine since the collapse back in December, I'd just put it down to the obvious factors. *I'm a bit older, I've got two kids now not one, I just need to take it easier this time*, I told myself.

A couple of days after his strange behaviour in the snow, Billy started acting weirder and weirder. On the Monday, he did something he had never done to that point and has never done again since. He went to the toilet in the house.

We had never had a litter tray because we'd never needed one; both Billy and Toby always went outside to do their business. Today, for some reason, Billy had decided to head into the corner of the kitchen and just do a wee on the tiled floor. I caught him red handed, so to speak. When I saw him standing next to the pool of orange-tinted liquid on the clean tiles I was shocked and really annoyed with him.

'Billy, you messy boy,' I said.

It was completely bizarre and out of character. He was a typical cat and was very clean otherwise. That wasn't the end of his odd behaviour, however. That same evening he jumped up on to the worktop, again, something that he'd never done before.

'Shoo, get down, Billy,' I said, scolding him.

He trotted off and then began running manically up and down the stairs. When I stepped into the hall-way and watched him for a second, he gave me a strange look then ran out into the utility room where, again completely unexpectedly, he jumped up on the work surface there.

I didn't have time to chastise him this time because the phone rang. It was my mum.

'Billy is behaving really weirdly,' I told her after we'd caught up on our main news.

'Has he got fleas?' she said.

We'd had a cat that had got fleas once and I could still remember how unpleasant it was.

'I'll check but he shouldn't,' I said. 'He's always outside. Maybe he's picked something up rubbing against something outside.'

I took a look after finishing the phone call but there was nothing.

The next day he was equally odd. During the day he started pouncing on my feet again, appearing suddenly from various nooks and crannies in the house and just jumping out. It was slightly sinister, as if he was stalking me. He was behaving like Pippa had begun to do when I was on the phone, coming up and mithering me, 'Mummy, mummy'. He was clearly trying to get my attention in some way but why? I had absolutely no idea.

That night, the Tuesday night, he kicked it up a gear. It was unbelievable. Chris had gone upstairs for a bath and the kids were in bed. I was sitting in the kitchen doing a puzzle when I heard a loud crash. I went to the front door and looked upstairs but couldn't see anything. Then I heard the crashing again.

Eventually I spotted that Billy was at the back door, crashing with his paws at the handle.

'Come in then,' I said, opening the door.

But he just ran off into the dark.

I was worried by now. I was beginning to imagine all sorts of things; that Billy had been driven mad by brain disease or that he'd caught some sort of rabies.

'No, it won't be anything serious. Maybe he needs a visit to the vet,' Chris said, calming me down as he came into the kitchen. 'Just in case he's caught something nasty out and about in the woods.'

I didn't have a chance to reply. All of a sudden we heard a dull thud, as if something was colliding with the door again.

I went down to the back porch and opened the door once more. This time Billy came inside the house.

'What on earth is a matter with you? Are you hungry?' I said.

I put some meat in a dish but he wouldn't eat. He was still jumping around weirdly, colliding with things and trying to gain my attention somehow. Why on earth had he suddenly fixated himself on me? I couldn't fathom it.

The following day, Wednesday, I began to feel quite poorly. I called Aberdeen hospital and they advised me to come in as a precautionary measure. They knew about the problems I'd had with Fraser and Pippa as well as the collapse I'd had prior to Christmas so they didn't want to take any chances.

Fortunately the children were in bed so a neighbour agreed to come in and keep an eye on things.

Without going into all the gory details, I knew fairly quickly that I was having a miscarriage. We headed off to hospital at 8 p.m. and by 9.30 p.m., within about 10 minutes of my arrival, a doctor told me that I had lost the baby. The staff were really professional but there wasn't anything they could have done.

I was devastated, in a state of shock. For a while it didn't really sink in.

The worst thing was that the specialist ward for women who had suffered miscarriages was closed because of staff shortages. So I had to go into the ward where the other maternity ward patients had successfully given birth to their babies. They put me in a room on my own but it didn't really help to ease the pain. My overwhelming feeling was that I didn't belong there. I didn't want to be around women with babies. Mine was gone and I wanted to get home to Fraser and Pippa, my two children.

They kept me under supervision until around 3 a.m. to make sure the bleeding had tailed off. They wanted me to stay in for a scan the following morning but by that point I'd had enough. I just wanted to go home. I really needed to be with the children.

Chris was worried about me and asked me to stay but in the end he saw that it was causing me more harm than good to stay in hospital. He could tell how upset I was.

So we explained the situation to the registrar. They understood that we lived in a remote community and that I had children who needed me. If there was more heavy snow, as forecast, I could have got stuck there for four or five days. So they agreed to discharge me.

Chris drove me back in the wee small hours. It was a strange journey; neither of us was able to say very much as we wove our way through the bleak landscape. There wasn't that much to say in many ways. We were both hurting too much.

I got home and went to bed. Sleep came easily because I was exhausted. The next morning Chris stayed home after he'd made the wretched call to tell his boss what had happened. As I heard him explain the events of the previous night I just felt numb, I couldn't cry.

For the first day I felt an unbelievably powerful sense of guilt; this must have been my fault. All sorts of thoughts raced around inside my head. Perhaps I shouldn't have lifted Pippa into the car so often.

Perhaps I should have taken more exercise or less exercise. Perhaps I should have weighed less. I punished myself for the whole day.

The following day I received some flowers. I should have appreciated them but instead they were the trigger for the floodgates to open.

I was furious. How could flowers ever make it better? I had lost my child, I had suffered a miscarriage. How I hated that word. It seemed a word devoid of emotion.

Looking back on it now, I can see that I was experiencing grief I had never felt before. And in amongst that grief were so many other emotions: anger, self-loathing and all sorts of other negative feelings from years before. Suddenly, as I lay there, they all came knocking at the door.

I stayed in bed for a day or two, I can't recall exactly how long. Slowly I realised that I couldn't carry on like this. I knew I had to cope. I had two children to look after.

I didn't cry in front of the children, I kept going, because that's what you do, of course. All those horrible clichés raise their head: 'time's a good healer', 'you move on', 'everything happens for a reason'. Except they weren't at all helpful, useful or relevant to what I was feeling.

They were difficult days but we muddled through. Sometimes I would be fine, sometimes not.

I was still going through the anger phase so I oper-
ated on a short fuse for quite a few weeks. I was
snappy and moody with everyone; Chris, Fraser,
Pippa, everyone. It took its toll physically too. I
looked washed out, I was tired, exhausted really. I
felt like I had done ten rounds with a heavyweight
boxer. I looked sad, even when I smiled.

Eventually, after some time passed, I was able to
put into perspective what had happened. But that
little piece of grief will always be with me.

It took Chris and me a while to regain our
equilibrium.

We'd resisted the temptation to think too far ahead
but we'd naturally talked in principle about things
like schools and maybe moving to a bigger property.
So it was hard to get back to day-to-day life knowing
that those plans had to be abandoned, possibly
forever. I was still in my thirties but, realistically, the
chances of me having another child were fading. It
was hard to accept but it was true.

It was strange but it was a couple of weeks after the
miscarriage that it dawned on me what had happened
with Billy.

It was a little like a cartoon again, as if a light bulb

had come on in my head. 'Hold on a minute, all that bizarre stuff he was doing has stopped completely,' I said to myself one day, as I sat in the living room watching him rolling around with Fraser.

Suddenly I put two and two together; Billy must have known something. There was no other explanation. Why was he jumping around so crazily during those three days before I miscarried? He had been with us for a year and a half now and had never shown me much interest at all. Why had that suddenly changed?

This time, I knew I was really pushing things to the boundaries of possibility. There was evidence that cats could pick up on illness but this really was a super-power too far. I'd heard of people having a sixth sense but this was way beyond that. Picking up on a miscarriage – this was a sixteenth sense. I was still very fragile emotionally and didn't want people to think I'd flipped so I didn't mention it to anyone, not even Chris.

The good news was that Pippa and Fraser kept me more than busy. As spring came and went, there was so much to do – and so many decisions to make. The biggest was Fraser's future at school. He had turned five in March 2013 so we had to submit a formal application for Fraser to start primary school that August. It was the sort of decision a lot of parents in big cities agonised over. Will my child get into the best school? Will my child get into any school?

Fortunately we didn't face those kind of concerns. There was no chance whatsoever of a school being over-subscribed, quite the opposite in fact. There was more chance of rural schools in the Highlands closing because of empty classrooms. And, given Fraser's progress, the prospect of him needing to go to a 'special school' had receded to such an extent that a local school was now legally obliged to take him under Scottish law. So, for us, the decision boiled down to a simple choice: Ballater School or Crathie.

Chris and I had already made that decision. Indeed, if we'd had our way, he would have started at Crathie full-time already. Not everyone agreed, however.

In the run up to the application going in, I had an assessment with Fraser's new educational psychologist. It was held at Ballater School with his nursery teacher. The educational psychologist said he was pleased with Fraser's progress and, amongst other things, mentioned how his social skills had improved.

As the meeting progressed, it became clear that both of them felt very strongly that Fraser should remain where he was and go to Ballater School in August. Their argument was that it would suit him better because the larger class sizes would offer more stimulation and help his social skills. As each of them made their cases, I sensed that they were really leaning on me to do this.

I am not someone who can be steamrollered into making decisions, especially ones I don't agree with, so I stood my ground. In fact, I saw red and got really cross with them. I can't remember the exact words but they were along the lines: 'I am Fraser's mother and I know what's best for him. He is going to Crathie in August. End of story.'

The meeting left me seething. Chris looked a little sheepish when I told him what had happened; he knew me and my temper.

That evening I kept replaying the meeting in my mind, wondering whether I'd been too strong and too opinionated. The neurotic worrier in me began to wonder whether I'd somehow blotted my – and therefore Fraser's – copybook? Had I gone over the top? Did they think that I was a stroppy parent? Was I still emotionally vulnerable after the miscarriage? The guilt started to creep in but I didn't let it take root. I couldn't afford to.

I'd come so far with Fraser since August 2009. Back then I was told that his needs were too specialist for a normal school. But now, thanks to all the work Chris and I had put in and the help of some extraordinary people, he was able to do so much more than would have seemed possible back then. I had to make the right decision and Crathie was that right decision.

It was time to look to the future. I had to try to put the sadness of the early part of the year behind me. I had to start planning for the start of Fraser's proper schooling in mid-August. We put the application for Crathie School in the post.

Chapter 18

Go Away

It was a bright, sunny July afternoon and I was in the garden hanging out some washing when I heard Fraser chatting merrily away.

I couldn't quite work out what he was saying but picked out the words from one of his favourite bedtime stories, *My Chunky Friend*, about an orangutan.

I poked my head around the corner and saw him and Billy sitting on the cinder path leading from the house.

Fraser had dragged the doormat from the porch out to sit on and had his book open on his lap. Billy was lying there, soaking up the sunshine and wagging his tail.

I just watched them for a few moments as Fraser jabbered away, occasionally looking at Billy or chastising him gently.

'Stop that, stop wagging your tail,' he would say, before resuming his story.

After a few moments, he folded up the book, picked up his mat and headed back towards the house.

'There, did you like that story, Billy?' he said.

I couldn't help smiling.

Fraser hadn't learned to read properly yet but he absolutely loved books. I think, again, they appealed to the orderly nature in him. Books were organised into a beginning, a middle and an end.

His love for stories was largely down to Chris, who had read him a bedtime story every night since he was two or three years old. Fraser simply adored having his father read to him and he didn't care if he was read the same story, night after night. In fact, he preferred it that way. Chris often read the same story over and over again for a fortnight. Fraser would never get bored.

He was picky about the books he liked, naturally. He didn't like stories that were too wordy and particularly loved stories that rhymed. He was fond of writers like Nick Sharratt and books like *Don't Put Your Finger in the Jelly Nelly*, *Shark in The Park*, *Ketchup on Your Cornflakes?* and a particular favourite, *Chocolate Mousse For Greedy Goose*. That one made him laugh like a drain every time he heard it. He loved the rhyming language, lines like 'macaroni says Shetland pony' or 'where's the meal said hungry seal?'. He had learned to memorise the lines of his favourite books parrot fashion. He would then recite them to anyone who was prepared to listen.

The one thing that had changed in the last couple of years was that Billy would often lie with them, as if he was listening to the story too. It was remarkable really. If Chris was reading, Billy would never get up and walk away.

But Fraser reading to Billy was a new development. It couldn't have been better timed with Fraser due to start learning to read formally when he began full-time school in a few weeks' time.

Of course, it was the sort of thing that I should have shared with an educational psychologist. It's well established that children can learn a lot simply by memorising the images of the words they see. They can deduce quite a bit from the shape and length of the words and the number of words on the page. It was a really positive thing. But, once again, I decided against it. They'd think that I was bonkers, imagining that my son was learning to read by reciting memorised stories to his cat. But it didn't bother me, I knew it was having an impact and that was all that mattered.

To me, this was just another little positive sign that

Fraser was ready to take the big step up, that he might, just might, thrive when he started at 'big school'.

That day was now just a few weeks away.

We were trying to keep it low key and not make a big deal of it. I'd ordered his official Crathie school uniform at the end of June. It was only a Fred Perry style top, a sweatshirt and a fleece, all bearing the school logo but it was still a lovely moment when it arrived and I got Fraser to try it on. He looked so smart and grown-up.

Of course, Fraser being Fraser, there were issues. The main one was the trousers he'd wear with his uniform. He had tried on one pair and told me they were too itchy and made his legs feel like 'they were on fire' so I had to find an alternative.

I didn't want to get him something radically different from the school uniform, even though they weren't super-strict about dress code at Crathie. He stood out enough already.

My long-term plan was to slowly ease him into proper school trousers but, in the meantime, I'd gone on a special shopping expedition while visiting my mother in Essex. We'd spent an entire day traipsing around the Lakeside Shopping Centre. It felt like we'd visited every single shop before we eventually found the right ones, some soft, Cargo style trousers with a soft, sweat-shirt style material lining.

As part of our strategy to keep things low key, Chris and I hadn't talked about school too much during the summer holidays. Inevitably, given that the school was a short drive away from us and was visible on the main road to Ballater and beyond, it was never far from Fraser's thoughts, however.

Predictably, he would veer between bouts of excitement and anxiety. Often he would begin each day by asking 'am I going to school today?' or 'what will I be doing at school?' He'd stand there flapping his arms or with his arms behind his back, rocking on his heels. But at other times he'd reel off a list of questions with a really concerned look on his face.

'What time will I start school?'

'A quarter to nine in the morning, Fraser.'

'What time will I finish?'

'About five to three in the afternoon.'

'How long is playtime? Will the bell go off?'

It could go on for quite a while like this.

Given the trouble we'd had when Fraser had started at Ballater school, our biggest fear was another serious shift in his behaviour. We'd only just recovered from the way he'd behaved in the run up to changing nursery last year. Neither Chris nor I felt like going through that again.

As August loomed the finishing line seemed in sight. I began to make plans for his first day at school, midway through the month. I really should have learned that lesson by now because, of course, it was then that the absolute worst thing imaginable happened. Fraser fell out with Billy.

One of the great advantages of the old, private nursery was that it remained open throughout the summer. The state school, on the other hand, shut its doors for six weeks which meant I had Fraser at home for a month and a half. After almost the entire month of July with Fraser at home 24/7 I'd become really strung out so Chris's mum had stepped in and offered to take him for a week or so, if I was willing. She doted on him and was also very well trained in dealing with special needs people through her work so I was more than happy for him to travel up to the coast.

He'd been there a couple of times before, of course, but only for a few days at a time. I wasn't sure how he'd cope with a week away and, as I suspected, it was a mixed success.

Fraser enjoyed staying with his grandmother and loved the attention she gave him so he was fine for the first couple of days. But then she and her partner tried to take him on a day trip. That's when things turned difficult.

Chris and I had given up on day trips a long time ago; there were always so many issues. Fraser couldn't go to public toilets because of the noisy fans. Restaurants and cafes were also no-go zones because of the noise the various cappuccino makers, ice crushers and microwaves made. There were always a myriad other issues and it had simply become exhausting.

Chris's mum was determined to try, however, and had planned a day trip up to Aviemore, high in the Grampians.

Bless her, she'd had a whole itinerary worked out. Fraser was going to go on a steam train, then the funicular railway that went up the side of the mountain. They were going to finish it all off with a visit to the reindeer park. But they didn't achieve any of it. When they got to Aviemore, Fraser had a meltdown and they had to turn around again. By the time they got back to the coast, they had been driving for four and a half hours. They had never left the car and only eaten a sandwich each.

Chris's mum was very disappointed and upset by this but there was nothing I could say. We had come really far with Fraser but there were aspects of his life that hadn't changed and perhaps never would. We'd already been warned that some facets of this behaviour would carry on until puberty at which point anything could happen. That was a prospect that filled me with dread, to be honest. The thought of a six foot Fraser, bawling his head off at me was too much to bear. I batted it away whenever it entered my head.

Anyhow, when Fraser came back from his grandmother's he was quite stroppy, moody and generally unco-operative.

'I don't want to do it,' he began to say to me if he didn't fancy doing something.

He'd protested at stuff in the past, of course, but there was a rudeness to him suddenly. It was as if he had discovered a new, more mature way of venting his anger. He was also being unpleasant to Pippa.

We wrote it off as a minor blip, one of those strange, often inexplicable – but hopefully brief – phases that Fraser was capable of going through from time to time. But then it escalated. And in a really bad way. Suddenly Billy became the focus for his anger.

I first picked up on it one afternoon when I noticed that Billy wasn't lying on the carpet with Fraser while he watched television.

'Where's Billy, Fraser?' I asked him.

'Fraser doesn't like Billy anymore,' he said very matter-of-factly.

I was startled.

'Why don't you like Billy anymore, Fraser?' I said.

'Just don't like him,' he said, sulkily.

My initial reaction was to wonder whether it was

because they'd been separated for a week. But that didn't make much sense. They had been apart before and were usually even closer when they were reunited. Absence makes the heart grow fonder and all that.

A more plausible explanation was that Fraser was cross with him. During the summer, Billy had started hopping over the fence and playing with the two children next door, a pair of girls, one of 18 months and another aged five.

I'd noticed he was sometimes cool and distant with Billy afterwards but I'd not really taken it too seriously.

A day or two after his first outburst, however, I saw that it had actually become a big issue. Fraser was in the Wendy house that we'd built there when a ball came over the fence from next door.

'Can we have our ball back please?', the elder of the girls asked, appearing at the low fence.

Fraser didn't engage with her at all which I thought was, again, very rude.

'Of course,' I said. 'Here you go.'

When I tossed the ball over the fence, Billy jumped over with it.

'Oh hello, Billy, have you come to play?' the little girl said.

The look that flashed across Fraser's face was telling. It was as if someone had told him the tooth fairy didn't exist or that the world no longer contained any washing machines.

He knew I was taking in what was going on, so turned and looked at me.

'I don't care, he can go and live next door,' he said rather petulantly before skulking back into the Wendy house, shutting the plastic door behind him with as much force as he could muster.

This pattern went on for four or five days, during which time his mood remained quite unpleasant.

It threw me into a complete panic. It couldn't have happened at a worse time really, less than a week before Fraser started at full-time school. Our number one priority was to keep things as calm and routine and happy as possible at home – Billy was absolutely central to this. In fact he was the key to dealing with the inevitable hiccups that would arise in the days and weeks ahead.

If Fraser and Billy were no longer friends it would almost certainly mean trouble for us. It was already destabilising Fraser and would only do so even more once he was at school when every little issue would be magnified a hundred times.

It was so depressing. Again, I felt like a crazy person, worrying so much about my son's relationship with his cat. But, instinctively, I just knew it was bad news and was thrown into a complete funk by it, mostly because I had no idea what to do. How did you tell a cat and an autistic boy to kiss and make up? I'd read a lot of books by now but I was pretty certain there wasn't a chapter on that particular conundrum.

Things reached breaking point one evening. Fraser was sitting watching television when Billy slid in from outside and positioned himself on the carpet. It was a routine that they'd been through almost every day since Billy had arrived: television time was Fraser and Billy time. But not tonight.

I happened to be in there, reading the newspaper and having a cup of tea while dinner was cooking in the oven.

'Go away,' Fraser said, turning around and making a shooing movement with his hands.

Billy didn't move, so he raised his voice.

'Billy. Go away,' he said, much louder this time.

Again, there was no reaction. So Fraser slid backwards and placed his face within a few feet of Billy. He then roared at the top of his voice.

'GO AWAY.'

Billy jumped, as anyone would have done. He picked himself up and just headed straight for the cat flap.

'Fraser,' I said, shocked at the ferocity of his words. 'What has Billy done to you?'

He just looked at me, really angry, then put his hands over his ears and lay on the floor.

Chris was as upset as I was when I relayed what had happened to him later that night.

'I'm going to have to give him a talking to,' he said.

'I think you are,' I said. 'You know he listens to you.'

Chris is one of those quiet, authoritative fathers who doesn't raise his voice. But when he speaks he means it and Fraser knew it.

So that evening after bath-time, before he read Fraser his story, Chris sat him down in his bedroom and explained the situation. I knew when it was over because Fraser appeared with red eyes.

'Daddy is being mean to me,' he said.

'No he's not Fraser, Daddy is trying to help you,' I said, showing that all-important solidarity that parents have to display at such times.

Chris came down a few minutes later.

'What did you say?' I said.

'I told him that Billy was a special cat and he loved him very much. But if he was going to ignore him and not be very nice to him then he would be upset and he wouldn't be his friend anymore,' he said.

'OK. How did he take that?'

'He didn't say much. So I told him that he wouldn't like it if Billy did the same thing to him. That's when he started crying.'

'Oh well, I think you got the message across. It's up to him now. We can't force him to be friends with Billy,' I said.

'Couldn't have been timed worse though, could it?' Chris said. 'He's going to have problems when he starts school. We will be back to two hour screaming sessions again I guess.'

We both sat staring at our dinners, wondering where things might head from here. We didn't have to wait too long to find out.

The following morning, Fraser seemed anxious to see Billy.

'Where's Billy?' he asked repeatedly at breakfast.

Chris raised an eyebrow at me, which didn't need any interpretation. I was thinking the same thing. He wanted to kiss and make up. Unfortunately, I sensed he had missed his opportunity.

I'd heard the cat flap clanging very early, before any of us had got up and there was no sign of Billy either inside the house or outside in the garden, which was unusual. He hadn't missed a breakfast with Fraser for a while.

'I don't know, Fraser,' I reassured him. 'Maybe he's out playing already.'

'Hmmmm,' he said, looking downcast.

Chris winked and nodded at me. His message had definitely got through.

'They'll be the best of pals again by teatime,' he said quietly, giving me a peck on the cheek and heading off to work.

Fraser had to go to play group at Crathie that

morning and didn't return until lunchtime. There was still no sign of Billy, which put him in a foul mood.

Chris had popped home for lunch.

'No sign of Billy?' he said.

'Nope.'

'Oh God, you don't think he really has run off do you Louise?' he said. 'I think I said he'd go away if he carried on ignoring him but I didn't think it would actually happen.'

It was a strange role reversal. It was normally me who hit the panic button first, not Chris. I think he felt guilty because he'd given Fraser a dressing down the previous night.

'No, come on, he's been missing for a lot longer than this before. He's probably just taking it all out on some poor creature in the pine forests.'

'Hope so,' he said.

It was late afternoon and I was in the kitchen starting the children's tea when I heard Fraser's raised voice somewhere near the utility room.

'Mummy, Mummy, Billy's not well.'

On the one hand I was hugely relieved that he was back but on the other, there was something about Fraser's voice that didn't sound right.

'How do you know he's not well, Fraser?' I said, from the kitchen.

'He's very dirty,' Fraser said.

'What do you mean very dirty?' I said, stopping what I was doing and heading to investigate.

Arriving in the utility room, I was shocked by what I saw.

Billy looked like he'd been down a coal mine or something. He was caked in dark soot or earth, I wasn't sure what. Not only that, he looked distressed and shaky. He was also unsteady on his feet.

I knew he was in a bad way so called the vet immediately. With the Queen due to arrive in a few weeks' time Chris was really busy on the Estate and wouldn't want to be disturbed so, if necessary, I'd have to take Billy to the vets with the children in tow.

Once again, a million irrational thoughts rushed through my head. *What if Billy was really ill? What if, heaven forbid, he died? How would Fraser react?* Fortunately, when I rang the vet he was a lot more level-headed than me. He quickly hauled me back to reality and told me that he needed me to make a couple of checks.

'They will help me decide if he needs emergency treatment or not,' he said.

First he asked me to feel Billy's limbs for cuts or bleeding or any sign of distress. I gave each of his legs a gentle touch and got no reaction, which was encouraging. When I touched his head, however, it was a different matter. He let out a really loud screech. I could see there was a cut there.

'That will need cleaning but it doesn't sound like

an emergency,' the vet said when I described it to him. 'OK, good, now I need you to check his eyes, ears and throat,' he said.

I did so but couldn't find anything wrong.

'And how's his breathing? Is he coughing or spluttering or wheezing at all?' he asked.

'No,' I said.

'Sounds to me like he has fallen down a coal bunker or perhaps got trapped in a wood shed and some logs have fallen down on him and trapped him,' the vet said.

'So he'll survive then,' I said.

'Yes, he'll survive, Mrs Booth. But I'd recommend you bring him in for a check up soon, unless he takes a turn for the worse of course, in which case you should bring him over straight away.'

I put the phone down and breathed an almighty sigh of relief. I then grabbed an alcohol-free wipe and started running the utility room sink so that I could wash Billy.

Fraser had been standing alongside me throughout the phone call. I don't know whether it was that or simply the fact that he had found Billy looking so vulnerable but, for some reason, it was the trigger for him to dissolve into floods of tears. He was crying almost hysterically. He'd seen Billy unwell before. But this time, it really upset him.

'Don't cry, Fraser. Go and say hello to Billy,' I said, giving him a cuddle.

Billy had limped into a corner of the utility room, near the washing machine. Fraser carefully walked over to him.

'It's OK, Billy. You will be fine,' he said, crouching down and lying next to him on the floor.

I could see he was really concerned.

Fraser just sat there for a while, stroking his friend and sticking his head close to him, almost as if to make eye contact.

'Fraser loves Billy,' he said quietly, as they rubbed heads together. 'Fraser loves Billy.'

I gave him a thorough wash, cleaning the wound carefully and then moved Billy into the kitchen where we could keep a closer eye on him that evening.

Fraser remained there throughout, even missing out on *Tom and Jerry* for the night. He didn't leave Billy's side until bedtime and even then insisted that he sleep in his room. Chris carefully carried him up and lay him on the floor in case Fraser accidentally kicked him in the night.

As Billy recovered over the next couple of days the pair were like limpets, inseparable from dawn till dusk. In a way, it made the final countdown to 'big school' easy. Fraser had no time to worry about the bell or his uniform or who would sit next to him anymore; his only concern was Billy.

For a while, Chris and I tried to work out what had caused the rift. Perhaps it was simple jealousy about

Billy playing next door? Perhaps he was anxious about the changes ahead and had lashed out at his best friend? Whatever the truth, there was no question he had learned a valuable lesson. He hasn't fallen out with Billy again since.

Chapter 19

Big School

It was the night before Fraser was due to start full-time school and the house was a hive of activity. I was in the utility room, ironing and hanging his uniform and sports kit ready for the morning. Chris was outside tinkering with the car, which had been making a weird noise. We couldn't risk it not being fit for the school run the following morning.

Fraser and Pippa meanwhile were being entertained by my mum and dad who had travelled up a few days earlier.

They knew what an important moment Fraser's first day at 'big school' was for us and wanted to be there to share it.

Until now, our attempts to play it all down had been reasonably successful.

But as he ate his dinner this evening Fraser was very excited, especially as his grandparents from England were there.

'Fraser is going to big school tomorrow, granddad,' he said.

'I know. I wonder what you are going to do there,' he said.

'Reading,' he said.

'And numbers.'

We felt happy that he would be comfortable with both. His love of books and numbers was deep-seated and everyone who had seen him in recent months had talked about how bright he was. It was the social side of school that was our main concern.

He knew one or two of the older children who went to Crathie but he hadn't really hit it off with them on the rare occasions he'd seen them. The good news, however, was that he knew two other children who were 'going up' from the toddler group to the full-time primary school.

He hadn't said anything negative about them which, in Fraser's world, was a big positive, if that makes sense.

Because of all of this he went to bed happily, even though, with my mum and dad in Fraser's room, he was having to share with Pippa. Billy was there to help ease him into bed as usual.

The following morning Chris and I were up at silly o'clock. It was already a glorious, sunny Highland summer day and everyone was excited, well, except for Pippa who remained fast asleep when I entered her room and roused Fraser.

Mum and dad were still getting ready in Fraser's room so I took him into Chris and my room to get him dressed. He was a little apprehensive but all seemed fine, especially when Billy appeared at my feet.

Today, of all days, we knew that the breakfast ritual had to be spot on. So Chris had cut the Marmite toast into precise, triangular quarters and placed the yoghurt and squash on the table ready. He and I had a cup of tea while Fraser tucked in. Before long mum and dad had joined us in the kitchen.

We'd found a light rucksack that Fraser could safely carry and at about 8.30 a.m. we started making our move to the car. We took a photo of him outside the house before making the two minute drive across the Balmoral bridge to Crathie school. The two other children starting that day were there with their mums and dads too. They looked close to tears but I wasn't.

As Fraser walked up the steps with me I was determined that I was going to relish every second of a moment that, at one point, we had been told was impossible. Every now and again this morning I'd found myself casting my mind back to that fateful day in Aberdeen where the consultant had been so clear. Fraser will NEVER go to a normal school. She had been so adamant, so certain. And yet here we were.

So as I waved Fraser goodbye and headed back to the car where mum, dad and Pippa were waiting, I didn't feel remotely tearful. I didn't feel resentful or bitter either. I didn't even feel triumphant. I just felt happy and proud. Enormously proud.

They were only doing half a school day that day so we had three hours or so to fill before I'd be back to collect Fraser. Rather than going into Ballater we headed in the other direction, to Braemar, where there was a lovely playground for Pippa.

As it turned out my mum and dad enjoyed it just as much. While I pushed Pippa in a swing, my mum and dad rode a big zip-wire, screaming and shouting like they were 7 years old rather than 70 and 71. It was an indication, I think, of how elated everyone was about what had happened that morning.

We popped into a coffee shop afterwards. As we sat there, we couldn't help dwell on the past.

'There were times when your dad and I thought you'd never get to this day, Louise,' mum said.

'I know,' I said.

'The way he was when he was a baby, we thought he might end up in a special home or something,' my dad said.

'I know. So did we at one point,' I said.

Everyone was lost in their own thoughts for a moment. But then mum put her hand on mine and smiled.

'Your dad and me just want you to know that you and Chris have been amazing,' she said. 'Fraser couldn't have wished for a better mum and a better dad.'

It was at that point that the floodgates opened, all the pent up emotion of the past few days, weeks, months, probably years, came gushing out. It was embarrassing to be honest.

My mum passed me a handkerchief and I was soon having to dab away like a silly schoolgirl.

'Oh, sorry you two, I guess that was an accident waiting to happen.'

We headed back to Balmoral so that I could make Pippa some lunch. By the time I'd done that and put a load of washing in the machine, it was time to go and pick Fraser up. Dad volunteered to stay with

Pippa who was taking a nap so Mum came with me in the car to Crathie School. It was a glorious afternoon and, as we stood outside waiting, both of us watched a large bird of prey of some kind swooping along the length of the river then disappearing into the thick, dark woods on the other side. It was hard to believe that there had been a time when I'd regarded this place as a little slice of hell rather than heaven. That period, living in that remote cottage in the woods, seemed like another life altogether now.

Fraser emerged smiling but blissfully unaware of how excited we were to see him. In fact, he was pretty much oblivious to us, full stop.

'How did it go?' I asked him.

'OK.'

'Who did you sit next to in class?'

'Can't remember.'

'What lessons did you have?'

'Can't remember.'

Mum and I exchanged smiles. I'd probably been just as monosyllabic when she'd first picked me up from school.

The drive back home only took a few minutes so there was no time to interrogate him further in the car. As I pulled up outside the house, I saw all hope of talking to him for the next hour or so disappear. Billy was standing by the porch.

'Billy. Billy.'

Moments later they were lying on the living room floor, lost in their shared world.

'I've got the kettle on. Fancy a cup of tea?' my dad said, emerging from the kitchen.

'Please,' I said.

As we sat down we could hear a voice blending in with the building noise of the boiling kettle.

It was Fraser, talking animatedly to Billy. I managed to catch a couple of snippets.

'Fraser sat with Zara . . . ,' he said before his voice trailed off.

'Then Miss told a story . . .'

It was sweet but ever so slightly annoying too. I desperately wanted to know what he'd been up to.

'Dad, do me a favour and flick the kettle off for a second,' I said.

He nodded.

As the sound of the kettle faded and Fraser's voice came to the fore, all three of us tiptoed our way to the edge of the living room then stuck our heads through the door.

Our amateurish attempts to eavesdrop were soon rumbled. Spotting the unwanted intruders, Fraser leaned in closer to Billy and gave us a disapproving frown.

'Sssh, Fraser is talking to Billy.'

We all laughed and scuttled back to the kitchen.

Fraser settled into school remarkably well. Even when the 'bedding in' period came to an end and he started attending for a full day, from 8.45 a.m. to 2.55 p.m., he took it in his stride.

We had been worried that he might have issues with being given specific tasks to do but his teachers had no complaints. In fact, they told me he was prospering.

His first proper assessment after a month or so was glowing.

'He's very quick, he is picking up reading really fast,' one of his teachers said. 'It's a joy to have him to be honest.'

It was his social development that really blew us away. Almost immediately he began to make friends and play with other children, some of whom he'd known through the toddler group. Maybe it was because he had a sister at home but at first he preferred the company of girls and loved hanging out with a friend's daughters, Phoebe and Isabel. He even began going to their house, although I suspected part of the fascination there was the fact my friend had a flashy washing machine that he particularly liked. That was a habit that wasn't going to disappear in a hurry.

The most significant moment socially, however, came about ten weeks after he'd started school, early in November.

Slowly he'd become friendly with the boys at school. There were only five of them so it wasn't hard to get to know them. They were a mixed age group; Fraser was the youngest and the oldest was ten.

When one of them invited him to his birthday party after school one day Fraser said he'd like to go, which delighted Chris and me. He'd never been to someone else's house for a party before; it had always worried him too much. Not only that, he said he was going in fancy dress.

When the day came he arrived home from school as excited as I'd ever seen him. He was too fired up even to talk to Billy.

'I don't have time to talk now, I've got to get changed for a party,' he'd said, dashing upstairs. When I offered to help him get dressed, he informed me in no uncertain terms that he didn't need me.

'I can do it on my own,' he said.

I'd driven him over to the boy's house, fully expecting to spend an hour and a half there, keeping a quiet eye on Fraser. But when we got to the gates he again announced that 'he didn't need me' and that he could go in on his own. I went home for an hour, laughing to myself.

'Looks like you and I are redundant,' I'd said to

Billy, who was taking the opportunity to have a snooze in the washroom.

When I picked Fraser up at the end of the party, he was beaming. He'd clearly had a fantastic time. I was speechless – and absolutely over the moon.

Chris couldn't believe it when I told him what had happened.

We immediately began making plans for Fraser's sixth birthday the following March. The idea of throwing a proper party for a gang of his 'mates' would have been unthinkable a year or two earlier.

A couple of weeks later, he did something equally remarkable. I was getting him ready to leave for school one morning in mid-November when there was a knock on the door. I opened it to discover the school bus driver who had parked outside.

'Morning, I'm here to collect Fraser Booth,' he said, smiling.

It threw me completely. I'd planned for Fraser to start travelling to school on the bus in the New Year but somehow the wires had got crossed with the council.

'Oh, I don't know if he will come with you today,' I said. 'Give me a second.'

We'd started preparing Fraser for this but it was still way sooner than we'd planned.

'Fraser, do you want to go on the school bus today?' I'd said, expecting some reluctance at the very least.

He took a step outside. He saw one of his friends on board which made him happy but significantly, Billy was also there already, waiting for him. He had reacted the moment the bus had arrived, scampering down the stairs and out down the pathway. He was now waiting in the open gateway, as if encouraging Fraser.

He was already in his uniform and had his rucksack ready.

'OK,' Fraser said, heading towards the bus.

As he'd climbed the steps, Billy had jumped on to the fence.

'That's my cat Billy,' Fraser had said to the driver.

It was amazing. A year earlier, a situation like that would have inevitably caused a meltdown. Yet now he was taking changes like this in his stride.

We saw all sorts of other improvements too, in Fraser's language and confidence, for instance. Interestingly, he had begun to use the 'I' word rather than speaking about himself in the third person. This was a significant step because it meant he was becoming more self-aware. He even began talking about us going on a holiday after hearing about a school friend's trip to Center Parcs.

'Can we go there, Mummy?' he asked one day.

'Well, yes, why not, Fraser?' I'd said.

I knew several sets of goalposts were likely to have shifted by the time we got to next summer. We'd always face those; it was a fact of Fraser's autistic life. But, for a moment or two at least, I had allowed myself to be excited at the prospect of our first proper holiday as a family.

Going to school at Crathie each day was a real joy, not just because it was proving such a great, nurturing environment for Fraser but because it also brought me into contact with people who knew us well. When I'd first arrived in Scotland I'd felt like a real outsider but now, five years on, I felt really at home there.

Picking Fraser up one afternoon I saw another mum whose daughter was a similar age. They'd been at toddler group together over the years so she knew a lot about Fraser and his problems. She normally worked during the day so it was rare to see her at school.

'Hi, long time no see. How's he settling in?' she said.

'Great, actually. He's really enjoying himself.'

'Gosh, he's come on so much hasn't he?' she said, seeing him skipping ahead of me down the steps towards the car. It was a sunny afternoon so we stopped and chatted for a while. Fraser had let himself into the car and was content.

The lady worked in the health service and knew a fair bit about what I'd been through and some of the personalities that had been involved. I was fulsome in my praise for almost all of them.

'Quite a journey you are on Louise,' she smiled.

'And quite a way to go,' I said. 'If we've learned anything it's not to look too far ahead though. One day at a time.'

She smiled.

'Oh, and how is the wee cat? I saw that lovely piece in the paper a while back.'

'Oh yes, Billy, he's been a good friend to him,' I said, understatedly.

'From what I read in the paper about him, he's a good deal more than that.'

Of course, she was right.

When I'd first met this lady three or four years earlier I had been going through one of my regular periods of despair. Fraser would sometimes go to playgroup and just lie on the floor, hitting his legs with his arms or – more likely – endlessly spinning the wheel of whatever car or toy he could lay his hands on. He would spend some days in a corner doing absolutely nothing, interacting with absolutely no one. Well, except for me, with whom his main means of communicating was to scream until he was purple in the face. And yet here he was now, a happy, friendly and charming little boy, skipping his way home after a day attending a normal school.

Yes, a lot of people had played their part during these last five, tumultuous years. Yes, some very wise heads had guided us along our very rocky road. But Billy's role was crucial and his influence had been absolutely immeasurable. He hadn't just been a good friend, he had been what Fraser had predicted from the start; he had been his very best friend.

From that first evening there had been something magical, almost other-worldly about their friendship. Billy had the ability to enter Fraser's own, private universe, a place that none of us could penetrate. It had made that universe a less lonely place for Fraser but, not only that; it had encouraged him to venture out of it so that he was now more and more a part of our world.

The things Billy had achieved weren't miracles in themselves: helping Fraser to calm down when anxious, encouraging him to walk, to use the toilet and to read, but they were small steps. But added together, to me at least, they seemed to add up to a miracle. To me he was the rescue cat that rescued my son. We simply wouldn't have been where we were today without him.

What made it truly special was the fact that I knew Fraser felt that way too. He'd said so often, always in his own, unique way, of course.

Just a day or two before that conversation outside school, I'd been straightening out Fraser's room ready for him to move back in after my mum and dad had headed back to Essex.

I'd taken advantage of the peace and quiet to sort through all the paperwork that I'd accumulated over the years.

There was so much of it. I had thick, dog-eared files full of letters from various doctors, therapists, schools and education authorities. It had probably taken a small forest to provide the paper that Fraser had generated.

In amongst the formal letters, I stumbled across the old diary that had been compiled at his first nursery. I couldn't resist sitting on the edge of Fraser's bed and flicking through the pages, so many of which brought back bitter-sweet memories. There were comments in there that made me smile, others that made me well up. It was one particular entry, from March the previous year, which brought the tears rolling.

Towards the end of each day the nursery liked to get all the children to sit in a circle on the floor so that they could read, listen to stories or chat. At first Fraser had refused to join in, preferring to play by himself, but slowly this had changed. His diary was dotted with notes about his contributions to 'circle time' as they called it.

On this particular day they had been making

presents for Mother's Day, that coming weekend. With the help of the teachers, Fraser had made a sweet, little card with a picture of me on it. At circle time the children had sat in a ring, cross-legged on the floor speaking about what made their mummies so special.

I pictured the children gushing sweetly about how they loved their mum's cuddles or cooking skills, the way she tucked them into bed at night or cared for them when they were poorly. When it came to Fraser's turn, however, his message had been typically short and sweet.

'My mummy got me Billy,' he had told the group.

That said it all, really. I got him Billy. And I'm so glad that I did.

Acknowledgements

I have to thank so many people not just for this book, but for helping me over the past few, difficult years. First and foremost, Chris. Sometimes when I look back it beggar's belief what we have been through together. But I wouldn't change a single thing. You are my world. You have been and are amazing.

Mum and Dad, after fifty years of marriage you have set me the best example of how a loving partnership can overcome all the odds. Mum, you brought me up to believe anything is possible if you try hard enough . . . and you were right!

Mirabel and John, even when times have been tough you have been there for Fraser and he adores the time he spends with you.

I am fortunate to have shared the company of some truly inspirational people all of whom have collaborated to help us raise the most special little boy.

At Ballater Health Clinic: Jayne Mackenzie, Dr Moira Collins and Dr Douglas Glass.

At the Raeden Centre, Aberdeen: Staff and Doctor A Stephen.

At Stonehaven Child Development Team: Doctor Ai Lin Lee, Doctor Jane McCance, Linda Collyer, Marie O'Gorman, Kaye Cumming, Lindsey Kelly and Helen Singleton.

Orthotics: Lynne McEwan.

Educational Psychology: Elayne Steele and Stuart Bull.

At Rose Lodge Nursery Ballater: A heartfelt thanks to the very special ladies who played a massive part in taking care of Fraser and helping him integrate into a classroom environment. You were all really important to us and words don't seem enough to express our thanks Cath, Emma, Laura, Joanna and Charlotte.

At Crathie School: Lillian Field, Alison McCrory, Les Roberts, Susan Boyd, Duncan Woods and Maggie Skene – thank you for the wonderful work you have done so far with Fraser, your endless ideas

ACKNOWLEDGEMENTS

involving home appliances never cease to amaze me as does your complete and thorough understanding of his educational needs.

At Balmoral: I would like to thank the resident Factor of Balmoral Estate, Richard Gledson for the continuing support and understanding of Fraser's ever changing needs and for all the assistance we have been offered as a family.

Writing this book has been an adventure, one that I'd never have imagined possible. I have to thank a number of people for helping me.

At Aitken Alexander: special thanks to my agent Mary Pachnos, Sally Riley and the foreign rights team for taking me on, championing my story and helping us to – we hope – one day making 'The Mary' a reality. (They will know what I mean.)

At Hodder & Stoughton: I have really enjoyed meeting and working with Rowena Webb, Emma Knight, Bea Long and Emily Robertson. Thanks also to Ciara Foley for her excellent work in editing the manuscript.

I consider myself to have made a true friend in Garry Jenkins. Thank you for making sense of the drama, handling our story with dignity, your empathy and understanding of Fraser (and me) and most importantly for helping me to lay my ghosts to rest. You rock.

And finally . . .

At Cats Protection: I would like to thank Liz Robinson and all at Cats Protection. Liz understood from the start the companion we needed for Fraser, she knew Billy was right and we all witnessed the magic from the very start. Liz, I hope you now know just how important you have been in the development of Fraser and our peace as a family. Thank you so much for rescuing Billy and letting him come home to us.

Last but certainly not least, Mr Billy Booth. Where would we be without you? You are a maverick, a hero, a saviour and, most of all, you are Fraser's best friend.

Find out more at
www.facebook.com/FraserandBilly

An invitation from the publisher

Join us at www.hodder.co.uk, or follow us
on Twitter @hodderbooks to be a part of
our community of people who love the very
best in books and reading.

Whether you want to discover more about a book
or an author, watch trailers and interviews, have the
chance to win early limited editions, or simply browse
our expert readers' selection of the very best books,
we think you'll find what you're looking for.

And if you don't, that's the place to tell us what's missing.

We love what we do, and we'd love you to be a part of it.

www.hodder.co.uk